"This thin volume is full of insights into one of the world's most complex and important relationships. No other book presents such a variety of perspectives, options, and predictions about the 'power triangle' that binds and divides Turkey, Israel, and the United States."

—STEPHEN KINZER
Author of *Reset: Iran, Turkey, and America's Future*

"This short but smart book provides fascinating insights on why Turkey no longer gets along with Israel and the United States, who continue to have a 'special relationship' that has no parallel in recorded history. In particular, it shows that America's support for Israel's brutal treatment of the Palestinians is the main source of the troubles and that the situation is likely to get worse, not better, in the years ahead."

—JOHN J. MEARSHEIMER
Distinguished Service Professor of Political Science,
University of Chicago

The debate on the triangular relationship between the United States, Turkey, and Israel has been dominated by arguments stressing the Turkish government's 'Islamist ideology', the power of pro-Israel organizations and sentiment in American politics, and the challenges that the Arab-Israeli conflict poses to Israel. The contributions to this thought-provoking book reject these simplistic arguments and set out a compelling alternative . . . In *Troubled Triangle*, richly informed scholars and prominent experts from the United States, Israel, and Turkey provide new insights into the past and provoke fresh thinking about the present at a time when the popular uprisings of the Middle East have changed the political and strategic landscape of the region and a strategic alliance between the US, Turkey, and Israel is more critical than ever.

—GONUL TOL
Executive Director,
Center for Turkish Studies, Middle East Institute

# About

# Just World Books

## "Timely Books for Changing Times"

This title, like most of our titles, is being published first in paperback and will later be released in one or more e-book versions.

Just World Books produces excellent books on key international issues—and does so in a very timely fashion. Because of the agility of our process, we cannot give detailed advance notice of fixed, seasonal "lists." To learn about our existing and upcoming titles, to download author podcasts and videos, and to buy our books, visit our website: www.justworldbooks.com and check our updates on Facebook and Twitter.

Our first title was published in October 2010. By September 2011 we had published seven titles:

***America's Misadventures in the Middle East,***
by Chas W. Freeman, Jr., with a foreword by William B. Quandt

***Afghanistan Journal: Selections from Registan.net,***
by Joshua Foust, with a foreword by Steve LeVine

***Gaza Mom: Palestine, Politics, Parenting, and Everything In Between,***
by Laila El-Haddad, with a foreword by miriam cooke

***A Responsible End? The United States and the Iraqi Transition, 2005–2010,***
by Reidar Visser

***Food, Farming, and Freedom: Sowing the Arab Spring,***
by Rami Zurayk, with a foreword by Rashid Khalidi

***Where the Wild Frontiers Are: Pakistan and the American Imagination,***
by Manan Ahmed, with a foreword by Amitava Kumar

***War Diary: Lebanon 2006***, by Rami Zurayk

Upcoming plans include: a book on China by Chas W. Freeman, Jr.; an atlas of the Palestine Question, published in coordination with the Applied Research Institute, Jerusalem (ARIJ)—and more!

www.justworldbooks.com

# Troubled Triangle

# Troubled Triangle

## The United States, Turkey, and Israel in the New Middle East

William B. Quandt, editor

Charlottesville, Virginia

Typesetting by Jane T. Sickon for Just World Publishing, LLC.
Printed by BookMobile, USA, and CPI, UK.

**Publisher's Cataloging-in-Publication**
***(Provided by Quality Books, Inc.)***

U.S.-Turkish-Israeli Strategic Triangle (2011 : Center for International Studies, University of Virginia)
Troubled triangle : the United States, Turkey, and Israel in the New Middle East / William B. Quandt, editor.
p. cm.
Includes bibliographical references.
"Proceedings of a conference held by the Center for Internatinal Studies, University of Virginia, on April 1, 2011."
LCCN 2011936666
ISBN-13: 978-1-935982-10-4
ISBN-10: 1-935982-10-9

1. Middle East--Foreign relations. 2. United States—Foreign relations —Turkey. 3. United States—Foreign relations—Israel. 4. Turkey—Foreign relations—United States. 5. Turkey—Foreign relations—Israel. 6. Israel—Foreign relations—United States. 7. Israel—Foreign relations—Turkey. I. Quandt, William B. II. Center for International Studies (University of Virginia) III. Title.

DS63.18.U88 2011 327.56073
QBI11-600168

# Contents

# Note from the Center for International Studies

University of Virginia

*The Center for International Studies is proud to sponsor this important book on the domestic and international political forces shaping the critical triangular relationship among the United States, Turkey, and Israel. This work grew out of a conference held at the University of Virginia on April 1-2, 2011, and has been edited by Professor William B. Quandt, the convener of that gathering. It brings together first-rate political analysis from leading experts in Turkey, Israel, and the United States, who worked together to examine the complex interaction of domestic and international politics within and across their three countries, the ways in which such factors frame the range of politically meaningful choice in each of them, and in consequence the prospects for stable peace in the Middle East.*

*The scholars who contributed to this volume address important themes, including the contradictions of democratization, the role of Islam in post-authoritarian polities, the raw electoral logic of coalition politics in Israel, interest-group pressures in American politics, and the reaction of the United States to the defeat of historical allies in the region. Their treatment of these themes helps us to see that an effective understanding of this complex triangular relationship requires deep knowledge of the history, cultures, and political dynamics of each country, of the ways in which they interact with each other, and of the dangers and difficulty of artificially separating the study of domestic politics from that of international relations. In this respect, the book well reflects the central purpose of the Center for International Studies at the University of Virginia, which is to promote the understanding of world politics through teaching, outreach, and above all original research.*[1]

Gowher Rizvi
Vice Provost for International Programs &
Director, Center for International Studies,
University of Virginia

1. The Center for International Studies serves faculty, staff, and students from the University of Virginia and institutions around the world. Its mission is to provide a university-wide focus on global education and to link research universities, institutes, and scholars in the United States and abroad. The center convenes interdisciplinary faculty seminars on topics of global importance; supports faculty research, study abroad programs, and visiting international scholars at the university; encourages innovation in international curriculum design; and promotes the development of study abroad programs. For more information about center programs, please consult the center's website, www.virginia.edu/cis.

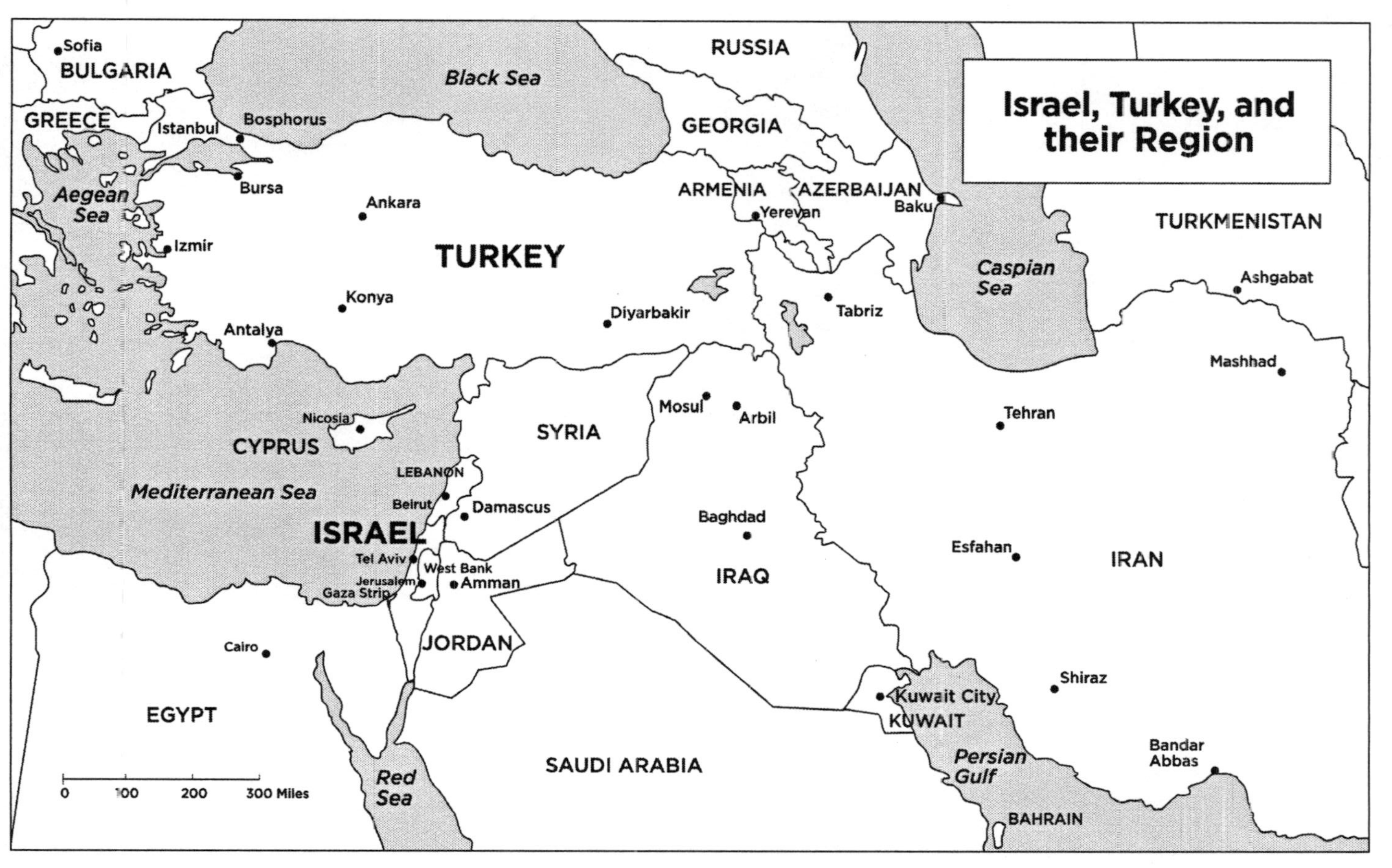


Map by Lewis Rector and © 2011 Just World Publishing, LLC

# Preface

*William B. Quandt, University of Virginia*

There was a time, not so long ago, when strategists in Washington imagined a strategic alliance, of sorts, linking the United States, Turkey, and Israel. The linchpin of the triangular relationship would be the United States, which had close diplomatic, military, and intelligence ties with each of the other two regional powers. Turkey and Israel had both sided with the United States during the Cold War; both were (more or less) democratic; and they shared a history of having been concerned with the threat of assertive Arab nationalism and radical Islam. So, to many observers there appeared to be a natural convergence of interests.

In reality, however, the triangular relationship has been troubled, particularly in recent years, as Israeli and Turkish foreign policy goals in the Middle East have diverged. And the United States has found it difficult to bring its two partners closer together, as has been evident since the *Mavi Marmara* affair (see below) in late May 2010.

To gain a deeper understanding of how each of these three countries—the United States, Turkey, and Israel—dealt with one another and with the rest of the Middle East during a period of dramatic changes, a conference was held at the University of Virginia in April 2011. Analysts from Turkey, Israel, and the United States addressed a range of issues involving the formulation of their country's foreign policy, the influence of domestic politics, and the likely trajectory for the future. Special attention was paid to Iran and the then-unfolding events of the Arab Spring.

The conference was originally structured around the notion of a "strategic triangle" involving the three countries. The basic idea was that each of the members of the triangle coordinated policies, to some extent, with the other two for mutual advantage. For a brief period from the mid-1990s to the early 2000s, this model seemed to describe the policies of the three countries. But most of the participants in the conference rejected the concept as a satisfactory description of the three-way relationship in recent years. Instead, each of the three countries has responded to changes in the Middle East with distinct policies that often put them at loggerheads.

---

*Arab-Israeli peace, which was explicitly not the central topic of this conference, had a way of working its way back into the deliberations.*

---

The reasons for these divergences were examined through two distinct lenses. First, analysts were asked to look at the strategic situation in which each country found itself. On the assumption that each country had a distinctive set of interests in the Middle East, it would be normal, according to realist logic, that their policies would not be identical. That indeed seemed to be the case. But foreign policy is not simply the product of realist calculations. Domestic politics also play a role, especially in these three electoral democracies. In fact, each contributor to this volume considered domestic politics to be an important part of the story of why all three countries pursued the particular course that they set for themselves. The analytical attempt to separate strategic considerations from domestic politics proved to be futile.

Although the contributors to this volume did not all agree on the reasons for the divergent policies, a number of points in common did emerge:

- Turkey's move toward a more independent and ambitious policy in the Middle East, which often sets its policies at cross-purposes with those of the United States and Israel, did not begin with the ascent of the Justice and Development Party (AKP) to power in 2002. Most of our analysts see the roots of Turkey's current policy in the growing economic power of Turkey, the realization in Ankara that integration into the European Union would be a long-term project at best, the urgency of confronting the instability caused by the Iraq War of 2003 and beyond, and a concern across a broad part of the Turkish political spectrum with the consequences of crises in Arab-Israeli relations since 2000.

- The particularly personal way in which Turkey's prime minister, Recep Tayyip Erdoğan, has spoken out about Israel in recent years is seen as less related to his Islamist sympathies than to specific events. Turkey, by all accounts, was playing a constructive role in mediating between Israel and Syria in 2008. This effort, not particularly welcome in official Washington, was emblematic of Turkey's "zero problems" with neighboring countries policy. Turkey had made great strides in patching up relations with Damascus, and saw a chance to play the role of mediator between Israel and Syria that had been left vacant by a lack of interest in the George W. Bush White House. In late December 2008, the Turks felt they were very close to bridging the gap between the two sides. They received Israeli Prime Minister Ehud Olmert in Turkey for talks, but just days later Israel launched the operation known as "Cast Lead" against the Hamas government in Gaza. This caught the Turks by surprise and brought their mediation effort to a sudden end.

  Turkish public opinion was solidly on the side of the Palestinians, and Turkey's prime minister apparently felt personally betrayed by the way the Israelis had behaved. And when given the chance to express his irritation in public, he did so in the presence of Israeli President Shimon Peres at Davos, Switzerland, in January 2009. This won him plaudits in Turkey, but not in Washington. As a savvy populist politician, Erdoğan realized that his tough stand against Israel was good for his popularity on the home front. And his electoral successes in 2010 (the referendum on constitutional reforms) and in parliamentary elections in June 2011 suggested that his reading of public opinion was accurate.
- The *Mavi Marmara* affair on May 31, 2010 came at a time when neither the Turkish nor the Israeli governments was in a mood to be conciliatory. Prime Minister Benjamin Netanyahu, elected in early 2009 and beholden to hard-line coalition partners, and Ehud Barak, his assertive minister of defense, were determined not to let the international flotilla of ships (including the *Mavi Marmara* with a number of Turkish activists on board) get through with its cargo of aid for Gaza. The actual encounter polarized relations sharply. Eight Turkish citizens and one Turkish-American youth were killed by Israeli forces as part of the operation to intercept the *Mavi Marmara*

in international waters. Turks were almost uniformly outraged and blamed Israel for a blatantly illegal act. They demanded an apology and compensation for the families of the victims. Israelis, by contrast, felt that the blame lay on the side of the Turkish activists aboard the *Mavi Marmara* and, behind them, the government that had allowed the ship to depart from Istanbul. The United States, already concerned by the strains between two of its rare allies in the region, could do little to ease the tension.

- U.S. policy, when looked at from the perspective of what we call in this volume the "troubled triangle," reveals a number of home truths. First, the United States has deep and complex relations with both Turkey and Israel, but only Israel has a strong base of support within the United States. Turkey and the United States are actually involved in a wide range of cooperative efforts—Afghanistan, Iraq, and most recently Libya—and President Barack Obama put Turkey at the head of the list when he visited the Middle East early in 2009. There he spoke of forging a "model partnership" with Ankara. But Turkey's "zero problems" with neighbors policy led to some awkward moments in relations with Washington. Turkey thought engagement with Iran would pay off politically as well as economically. And, perhaps overestimating its diplomatic clout, Turkey joined forces with Brazil to try to work out a compromise between Iran and the United States on the sensitive nuclear issue. For reasons that are still not entirely clear, the proposal that Turkey and Brazil put forward was not acceptable to Washington. This led to considerable irritation within the Obama administration, especially when Turkey refused to vote in favor of strong UN sanctions against Iran.

Some Americans saw Turkey's tilt toward Iran on this issue as part of a broader drift "eastward." The suspicion, sometimes explicitly stated, was that Turkey's Islamist government was pursuing an ideological agenda of solidarity with Muslim countries at the expense of its traditional Western partners and Israel. Turkey's openness to Islamist movements like Hizbollah in Lebanon and Hamas in Palestine reinforced this view. The contributors to this volume did not, on balance, give much credence to this view. And events since the conference—the crises in Libya and Syria—have not strengthened the belief that Turkish policy is heavily ideological. After some initial hesitation, Turkey has aligned itself with the NATO consensus on Libya, has called on Muammar Qaddafi to leave power, and has sharply criticized Syrian president Bashar al-Asad for his repressive policies. There were also signs as of mid-2011 that Turkey and Israel were preparing, cautiously, for some form of rapprochement. After all, the events of the Arab Spring had forced both of them to recalibrate their policies to some extent. But by September 2011, the effort to ease tensions had failed, as Israel refused to apologize for its actions against the *Mavi Marmara* and Turkey decided to downgrade its diplomatic relations with Israel and to suspend military cooperation.

- One of the benefits of looking at Middle East issues from the divergent perspectives of the United States, Turkey, and Israel is that we can better appreciate some of the complex developments taking place in the region. At some risk of overgeneralization, several points stand out. First, Turkey is capitalizing on its strong economy, its geostrategic location, its historical role, and its "soft power" to expand its influence in the region. Even those Turks who do not support the AKP are proud to see Turkey emerging as an influential regional power. Most of our analysts view Turkey as a natural rival for influence with Iran—especially in the Iraqi arena and, more broadly, in Arab public opinion. Turks are flattered to be seen as something of a model for the emerging democrats in the region—in sharp contrast to Iran, whose Shiite Islamic Republic has few admirers in most of the (mainly Sunni) Arab world. Retaining credibility in the Arab world by siding with the Palestinian cause is an important part of Turkey's regional strategy to offset Iran's influence. It does, of course, have the effect of annoying many in Washington and in Israel.
- While Turkey is expanding its horizons in the Middle East, Israel, it seemed to most of our analysts, is seeing its prospects for integration into the region slip away. Its formal peace agreements with both Jordan and Egypt remain intact, but the days of wide-ranging cooperation on regional issues are fading fast. Israel is as isolated within the region today as it has been at any time in the past three decades. It possesses undeniable military "hard power," but almost no "soft power" of relevance to the Middle East region. Its most important foreign relationship, by far, is with the United States, not with any of its neighbors. This growing estrangement from much of the region may lead Israel back to assigning some value to its relationship with Ankara.
- A final point worth noting is that Arab-Israeli peace, which was explicitly not the central topic of this conference, had a way of work-

ing its way back into the deliberations. The United States, at least at the rhetorical level, continues to assign the "peace process" a high priority, although in practice there has been almost no forward movement during the past decade. The Netanyahu government has been unable or unwilling to negotiate with its Palestinian adversary on terms that most of the international community supports—a freeze on settlement activity and the 1967 borders with mutually agreed modifications as a reference point.

Because of unquestioning support for Israel, especially in the U.S. Congress, and more generally in U.S. public opinion, Israel feels little pressure to change its hard-line policies. The stalemate has an adverse effect on Turkish-Israeli relations; the downturn in Turkish-Israeli relations has an impact on perceptions of Turkey in Washington; and thus the triangular relationship with respect to the Arab-Israeli conflict has a negative dynamic that has little to do with grand strategy and a lot to do with domestic politics. The potential synergies that might have developed as three strong democratic countries addressed regional issues with a shared strategic vision have thereby been lost or weakened.

As the United States disengages from its overextended, expensive role in the Middle East—Iraq and Afghanistan as the prime examples—and as Arab-Israeli peace remains elusive, we may expect continuing divergences among the three countries that are the subject of this book. Many uncertainties abound—especially with the upheavals in the Arab world—and all three countries in this "troubled triangle" will face tough choices. Whether they will do so with some remaining sense of common purpose is uncertain.

Iran may well be the issue that brings the differences among the three to the fore. Turkey, acutely aware of its geostrategic rivalry with Iran, but also seemingly convinced that consistent engagement is the best course of action, is unlikely to support muscular military policies aimed at Tehran. And yet these are the policies that many—not all—Israelis seem to favor. The United States, although deeply disappointed that its own efforts to engage with Iran have yielded no benefits, and under some pressure on the domestic front (from friends of Israel, among others), is nonetheless far from eager to consider a military strike against Iran's nuclear facilities. Diplomatic pressure and sanctions, and a hope for change from within Iran, are the preferred stance for the moment.

If Iran moves aggressively to acquire nuclear capabilities—by highly enriching uranium or actually producing a weapon—these underlying differences among the three countries will come to a head, potentially in a dramatic way.

These and other themes are discussed in subsequent chapters. Each author has written an original paper—most of which have been updated through mid-2011—and we include the remarks of distinguished commentators, as well as discussion and questions and answers, in order to give a sense of the richness of the deliberations sparked by these analyses. We believe that the perspectives offered here will help readers to understand many of the general contours of the "New Middle East" that is emerging before our eyes.

September 6, 2011

PART I

# Strategic Perspectives

*The original idea for this part of the discussion was that three richly informed scholars—one each from the United States, Turkey, and Israel—would examine the core strategic interests that each of their countries had toward the other two. For this purpose, I invited F. Gregory Gause, III, from the University of Vermont in the United States, Soli Özel from Kadir Has University in Istanbul, Turkey, and Shlomo Brom from the Institute for National Security Studies in Tel Aviv, Israel.*

*Gause brought to the discussion a broad familiarity with the strategic geography of the Middle East, especially the Gulf region and Saudi Arabia. His relative distance from the debates surrounding Israel and Turkey seemed like an advantage. I hoped he could bring his cool, realist perspective to bear—and he did.*

*The other two participants in this discussion were people more deeply involved in the day-to-day discussions of public policy in their respective countries. Özel is a well-known Turkish scholar who well fits the notion of a "public intellectual," frequently commenting on current affairs in a variety of public media. He is also a product of the American educational system and earned his PhD at Berkeley. He has a penchant for realist analysis and seemed like a good counterpart to Gause.*

*Brom, a former brigadier general in the Israeli Defense Forces, and now a prominent analyst at a well-known Israeli think tank, also brought to the discussion a deep familiarity with the broad strategic issues affecting the region.*

*Readers will see that there were some areas of convergent analysis, but also some significant divergences. Gause in particular found it difficult to avoid discussing the strong influence of domestic politics, not just strategic thinking, in explaining American policy. All three scholars, however, foresaw a future in which American influence in the region would be on the wane, Israel would be more isolated than before, and Turkey would be seeking a regional role in quite uncertain circumstances.*

*To comment on these three presentations, I invited three other prominent experts in geopolitical and strategic affairs. Ellen Laipson, the president of the Henry L. Stimson Center in Washington, D.C., is a specialist on the Middle East with extensive policy experience in the U.S. government. Philip Zelikow and Brantly Womack are both professors at the University of Virginia. Laipson was one of the first to raise the question of how to define a "strategic" interest, a question that reemerged numerous times throughout the day's proceedings. She helped move the discussion from the notion that states act on concrete national interests to an understanding that leaders define as "strategically important" things that they happen to care strongly about.*

*Zelikow also has had extensive experience in the U.S. government, including as executive director of the 9/11 Commission and as counselor to Secretary of State Condoleezza Rice in 2005-06. He combines his intimate, granular understanding of policymaking with the depth and thoughtfulness of a very serious historian. He introduced the idea that relations between states are "constructs," often best understood as metaphors that give meaning to discrete events, and often also serving to rationalize decisions that we make for reasons that are often opaque. He gave examples of how the very deeply "constructed" U.S.-Israeli relationship actually had less substance to it from an American perspective than the less-known and less-appreciated U.S.-Turkish relationship.*

*Womack is a political scientist whose areas of specialization are East Asia as well as "asymmetrical" international relationships in general. He gave a thought-provoking overview of how this triangular relationship centered in the Eastern Mediterranean looked to a generalist who concentrates on power relations among states of different strategic weights.*

*The individual contributions to this part of the conference were all of great interest. But in this session, as in those that followed, the interactions among the speakers, the commentators, and the broader group of questioners all added up to a rich and illuminating exchange of views.*

*~WBQ*

1

# The U.S.-Israeli-Turkish Strategic Triangle: Cold War Structures and Domestic Political Processes

*F. Gregory Gause, III, University of Vermont*

It is difficult to say that American policymakers ever viewed their relations with Turkey and Israel as part of a strategic triangle, with perhaps a brief exception in the late 1990s-early 2000s. Washington normally sees its relations with the two states through two different regional prisms. Israeli-American relations are seen as part of the more general Arab-Israeli or Middle Eastern strategic frame, and are deeply implicated in American domestic politics. Turkish-American relations during the Cold War had been viewed almost exclusively through a European lens, with occasional reminders that Turkey—because it borders Syria, Iraq, and Iran—had a role in Middle Eastern events. But Turkey was not seen as a major player in specifically Arab-Israeli dynamics. After the Cold War, Ankara had a role to play in Persian Gulf issues (in the two wars with Iraq) and, after 9/11, in Washington's engagement with the "Muslim world." This separation was expressed bureaucratically in Israel's location in the Near East Bureau (formerly Near East and South Asia) of the State Department and Turkey's in the Europe and Eurasian Bureau (formerly in Western Europe). The fact that the two regional allies got along fairly well with each other was seen, I would imagine, as a bonus, but not as a central feature of the bilateral relationships between the United States and them.

American relations with both regional states were largely, if not completely, defined by the Cold War international structure through the 1980s. In neither case did domestic political dynamics in the regional ally play that much of a role in the bilateral relationship. Although Turkey went through interesting changes and periods of intense domestic instability from 1946 through 1991, the strength of the Kemalist elite preserved a relatively consistent foreign policy stance toward the United States (obviously with some ups and downs, particularly over Cyprus). Likewise, domestic political change in Israel during the 1970s, when the Likud Party broke the Labor Party's monopoly over governance, did not change American-Israeli relations or views toward Turkey in any serious way. The end of the Cold War structural constraints on each of the three countries' foreign policies opened up space for domestic politics to play a greater role in how the three interacted, most notably in the case of Turkey but also in American-Israeli relations. It is the loss of that tightly constraining international structure that has allowed domestic political processes to become a more important, and more complicating, factor in how the triangular relationship works.

## The Cold War and the Triangle

From the American perspective, relations with both Turkey and Israel during the Cold War were viewed overwhelmingly through the lens of the global bipolar structure. Turkey was a valued ally against the Soviet Union. America's first Cold War policy was the Truman Doctrine, which involved American aid to Turkey (and Greece). Turkey was brought into the North Atlantic Treaty Organization (NATO) in 1951. It was part of America's "Northern Tier" strategy of containing the Soviet Union in the Middle East, joining the Baghdad Pact and then the Central Treaty Organization (CENTO) with Iran and Pakistan. It was one of the largest recipients, if not the largest, of American foreign military and civilian aid in the 1950s. The Turkish military was tightly joined to the American military, through the provision of American equipment and the officer corps' experience of training in the United States and service in NATO.

Turkey was a cornerstone of the American strategy of containment throughout the Cold War. This is not to say that the bilateral relationship was all kebabs and *raki* (or peaches and cream) during this period. The military interventions into Turkish domestic politics in 1960, 1971, and 1980 presented superficial problems for an American foreign policy that was, at least rhetorically, committed to democracy. The Turkish incursion into Cyprus in 1974 created real tensions and put at risk congressional goodwill toward Ankara. However, the overriding Cold War framework prevented an open break in the bilateral relationship, as both Republican and Democratic presidents sought to maintain good relations with Turkey despite congressional concerns. For the United States, Turkey was an important piece on the Cold War chessboard, not to be sacrificed for domestic political reasons—either American or Turkish.

Turkey's Cold War strategic view matched up almost completely with that of the United States. It saw the Soviet Union as both an historical (Russian) foe and an ideological enemy. The European and Western orientation of the Kemalist elite that dominated Turkish politics during this period also meant that there was strong coherence between Turkish domestic political orientations and its foreign policy preference for the American side in the Cold War. Even when the Democrat Party challenged the Kemalists in the 1950s, Prime Minister Adnan Menderes went out of his way to reaffirm the foreign policy tie to the United States, to placate his Kemalist critics in the military. In fact, the Menderes era probably marked the height of Turkish-American strategic cooperation. Turkey sent troops to fight with the United States in Korea, joined both the Baghdad Pact and CENTO, and mobilized troops along the Syrian border in 1957 as part of the failed American plan to bring down the Syrian government. Turkish leaders after Menderes might not have been as enthusiastic in their support for the United States, and some (Bülent Ecevit in the lead) did not hide their distaste for it, but good relations with Washington fit into Turkey's strategic imperative and its general domestic orientation toward the West.

Israel had a harder time at first finding its niche in American Cold War strategy. Although the United States supported the establishment of Israel diplomatically, it did little to aid Israel in its war of independence. Worried about how close ties with Israel would affect its effort to prevent the Soviets from making inroads in the Arab world, Washington kept the new state at arm's length in terms of strategic relations. The clearest manifestation of Washington's wariness about Israel's role in its global strategy was the Suez War of 1956. The Eisenhower administration condemned the British-French-Israeli attack on Egypt and put heavy pressure on the Israelis to give up their territorial gains in Sinai. However, by the 1960s, both the Middle East strategic picture and American politics were changing.

With Egypt, Syria, and Iraq increasingly drawn toward the Soviet side in the Cold War, Washington began to see Israel as a strategic asset against Soviet allies. Its victory in the 1967 War was an example of the superiority of American (and French) arms over those of the USSR. Unlike after Suez, this time the United States encouraged Israel to hold on to conquered Arab territories as a lever against its Arab neighbors. Close American-Israeli cooperation during the 1970 Jordanian crisis cemented the view in Washington that Israel was an important Cold War asset. Even the Arab oil embargo of 1973-74 did not shake that view, which reached its height during the Reagan administration. American military aid to Israel increased enormously, from the first major arms deals in the Kennedy and Johnson administrations to the substantial aid packages under President Richard Nixon, culminating in the post-Camp David level of aid that has been maintained ever since. While there were occasional periods of tension between the United States and Israel over the Arab-Israeli peace process, which took on a greater strategic importance for the United States after the oil embargo, during the remainder of the Cold War it was an article of faith in the American foreign policy establishment that Israel was a Cold War asset—or at least nobody in that establishment was willing to say otherwise.

The shift in American strategic relations with Israel from the 1960s was driven by Cold War dynamics, but it also squared nicely with the growing power of pro-Israel organizations and sentiment in American domestic politics. Although domestic political factors undoubtedly influenced President Harry S. Truman's decision to recognize Israel in 1948, it would be hard to argue that pro-Israeli groups exercised much clout in American politics during the 1950s. American aid to Israel in that period was minimal and President Dwight Eisenhower suffered no discernible negative consequences for his pressure on Israel after Suez. In the 1960s, the clout of Jewish pro-Israeli organizations increased, and in the 1970s and 1980s, Christian fundamentalist political groups came to take strongly pro-Israeli positions. Cold War dynamics and American domestic politics dovetailed in strengthening the American-Israeli strategic relationship.

There were some small reservations, immediately after independence, about close relations with the United States among the more left-wing elements of the constellation of Israeli parties that came to form the Labor Party. However, after Stalin's turn against Jews more generally in 1953 and the Soviet Union's alignment with Israel's Arab enemies during the 1950s, there was no discernible domestic opposition to close American-

Israeli relations. On the contrary, Israeli politicians strove to prove to their own constituents, and to the American audience, that they were more pro-American than their rivals. Opposition parties lambasted their governing rivals for real and imagined declines in the warmth of ties with Washington. Speaking good English became almost a requirement to be prime minister. Domestic politics was not really a factor on the Israeli side in the bilateral relationship.

Although the Cold War was the main driver of American relations with both Turkey and Israel, it is hard to speak of a strategic triangle during this time. Turkey did recognize Israeli independence in 1949, but had voted against the partition resolution at the United Nations in 1947. Turkey set up an embassy in Tel Aviv in 1950, as it was campaigning for NATO membership, but did not staff it at the ambassadorial level. Israel courted Turkey as part of its effort to establish good relations with non-Arab powers on the periphery of the Arab world (Iran and Ethiopia). In 1958, the two sides agreed to intelligence sharing and military consultations, but the agreement was kept secret at the insistence of Turkey. Turkey declared its opposition to the Israeli territorial gains in 1967 and, after the oil embargo of 1973-74, tended to side publicly with the Arab side on Arab-Israeli issues (in return, most Arab states supported Turkey's position on Cyprus). In 1980, Turkey publicly announced a "downgrading" of its relations with Israel, and in 1988 Turkey recognized the Palestine Liberation Organization's (PLO) declaration of an independent Palestinian state. There is no evidence that the United States pushed the two sides together in their bilateral relationship to any great extent. In general, during the Cold War Israeli-Turkish relations were correct but not that close.

## The Triangle after the Cold War

With the end of the Cold War, the overarching structural factor that defined the bilateral relations of the United States with Turkey and Israel was removed. While strategic issues were not absent from relations among the three after 1989, domestic political factors came to play a much greater role in bilateral relations, particularly between the United States and Israel and between Turkey and Israel. There was a brief period, in the late 1990s and early 2000s, when one could speak of a nascent triangular alliance among the three states. It fit in well with the American regional strategy of "dual containment" of Iraq and Iran at that time, and it fit the view of the

Kemalist military and civilian elite in Turkey about whom its friends and its enemies were, both at home and abroad. However, shifts in Turkish domestic politics, with the ascent of the Justice and Development Party (AKP) to power in 2002, put a brake on the development of the triangular relationship.

## Domestic Politics and American Views of Turkey and Israel

The United States' view of Turkey continued to be driven by strategic considerations in the post–Cold War period, but those considerations were substantially different from the Cold War period. In the 1990s, Turkey was seen as a major asset in the Middle East, because of its support for Washington in the Gulf War, and as part of the "dual containment" of Iraq and Iran during that decade. It was at the end of this period that there were the only real manifestations of an American-Israeli-Turkish "triangular alliance" (to be discussed below), and that was relatively short-lived. After 9/11, Turkey was still seen as a major strategic asset, but less because of what it could do and more because of what it was—a democratic Muslim country, from 2002 with an Islamist government (of sorts), that had good relations with the United States. Turkish democracy meant that Turkey would not play an active role in support of American Middle East policy (as demonstrated by the refusal of the Turkish Parliament to allow American forces to enter Turkey as part of the 2003 Iraq War, and as the AKP's policy toward Iran from the late 2000s confirmed), and led to tensions in Turkish-Israeli relations (to be discussed below). Turkish democracy and the AKP government in particular are viewed in Washington as a mixed blessing. But without the overarching structure of global bipolarity, Washington can be more comfortable with Turkey charting its own path—as long as that path is not overtly anti-American, like that of Iran—than it would have been during the Cold War.

Domestic politics is playing a much greater role in American-Israeli relations in the post–Cold War period. The end of global bipolarity robbed Israel of its major strategic argument for the "special relationship" with Washington—that it was a stalwart ally against the Soviet Union and its proxies in the region. The fact that the United States had to pay Israel to stay out of the Gulf War of 1990-91 brought this changed reality home in a very direct way. Although Israel and its supporters in the United States have argued in the post-9/11 period that the two countries share a common enemy in the global war on terrorism, the opposite argument—that close American relations with Israel increase anti-Americanism in the Muslim world—is at least equally compelling. The persistence of the Palestinian-Israeli conflict has helped Iran, the only major Middle Eastern state still following a "rejectionist" policy toward Israel, to increase its influence in the Arab world (though that is not the only factor). It is simply harder to make a strong argument that Israel is as strategic an asset for the United States as it was during the Cold War.

Despite that fact, there has been little change in American-Israeli relations. The two countries, occasional tensions on Arab-Israeli peace process issues aside, remain very close. Military and intelligence cooperation is very deep. Israel continues to be a major recipient of American foreign aid, far and away the largest recipient per capita and in many years the largest recipient in absolute amounts (in some years, depending on how one counts it, Iraq or Afghanistan or Pakistan might have received more aid than Israel). This can only be explained by a number of salient American domestic political facts: the generally positive American public opinion toward Israel, the variegated and extensive elite links between the two societies, and the active support of important political lobbies—both Jewish American and Christian—for the relationship.

One might even argue, counterfactually, that the end of the Cold War has made it less likely that the United States would exert extreme pressure on Israel regarding Arab-Israeli peace process issues, reflecting the dominant role domestic political considerations now play in the relationship. Imagine that the Syrian-Israeli negotiations of the 1990s that came so close to yielding a peace treaty had occurred during the Cold War. Would Washington have allowed the negotiations to collapse and lose the chance to turn a major Soviet Middle Eastern ally? We cannot know, but I doubt it. But in the post–Cold War period, the Clinton administration—despite the enormous commitment of its own time, resources, and prestige to the Syrian track—allowed the negotiations to fail. The strategic gains were not considered that substantial, so the willingness to pay the domestic price for increased pressure on Israel was not there. (Others will have a different view of these negotiations, blaming the Syrians for their failure, but the accounts by the participants indicate that the two sides were very close and that Prime Minister Ehud Barak backed away from the final necessary concessions at a crucial point in early 2000. When he was willing to reengage, the Syrians had become suspicious, and then Hafez al-Asad died.)

## Domestic Politics and Shifts in Turkish Views of Israel, the United States, and the Region

Domestic political factors played a determining role in Turkish views of both the United States and Israel during the post–Cold War period, and domestic politics pushed the relationships in different directions at different times. Two domestic processes are central here: the Turkish adoption of an export-led growth economic strategy under Turgut Özal, and the growing rivalry between the Kemalist elite and Islamist political forces that dominated the increasingly democratic (less military-controlled) politics of the country. The export-led growth strategy demanded good relations with the major world economic players, the United States and the European Union, but also pushed Turkey toward an opening to its Middle Eastern hinterland that had been largely ignored during the Cold War. Democratic competition and the rise of Islamist politics affected both relations with the United States and with Israel. Israel, in particular, became an element of domestic political contestation. The Kemalists, particularly in the military, increasingly saw Israel as a strategic ally against Islamist forces, both abroad and, indirectly, at home. Conversely, the AKP, responding to and leading public opinion, takes a much harder line against Israel, not only as part of its new regional strategy, but also as a rebuke to its rivals in the military.

Özal's reorientation of Turkey's economy required market access to Europe and, to a lesser extent, the United States. It also pointed Turkey toward greater involvement in the Middle East, a natural market for Turkish exports. The Gulf War of 1990-91 came at a propitious moment for Özal. His enthusiastic support for the United States (over the objections of many of his Kemalist generals) reaffirmed Turkey's strategic importance to Washington and also reintroduced Turkey into the politics of the Gulf region in a more direct way. The results of the Gulf War created a new element with respect to Turkey's Kurdish issue, drawing the military into northern Iraq on a number of occasions in the 1990s.

The new challenge presented to Turkey by Kurdish autonomy in northern Iraq was one reason why Turkey strengthened its relations with Israel in the 1990s. Focus on the Kurdish issue highlighted tensions with Syria, which hosted Kurdistan Workers Party (PKK) leader Abdullah Öcalan up to 1998, and so strengthened relations with Israel made sense in terms of regional power balances. Israel could also offer advice and training for the Turkish military on how to deal with a difficult border. But probably more central to Ankara's decision to warm up relations with Jerusalem was the increasing sense among the Kemalist elite that Islamist politics was a serious threat to its position, both at home and regionally. With the military, through the National Security Council, given a constitutional role in the making of foreign and security policy, Turkish foreign policy in the 1990s was insulated from public opinion considerations and even from the vagaries of electoral politics. The military could conduct foreign and security policy largely as they saw fit, and they moved to strengthen relations with Israel in an unprecedented fashion. In 1991, diplomatic relations were elevated to full ambassadorial level. The decade saw a number of bilateral agreements, visits by high-ranking officials of each country to the other, expanded trade and tourism (particularly Israelis visiting Turkey) culminating in a free trade agreement in 1997, and vastly expanded military cooperation. Even during the brief prime ministership of Necmettin Erbakan of the Refah Party, who had campaigned on a promise to break relations with Israel, military and economic cooperation flourished—a signal from the military that they were still in charge of Turkish foreign policy.

It was at this time that the brief flowering of the "triangular alliance" occurred. Joint Turkish-Israeli-American naval search-and-rescue exercises (Reliant Mermaid) began in 1998 (and continue to the present). In 2001, the three air forces held joint exercises (Anatolian Eagle) over Turkish airspace. The triangular alliance idea fit in well with the American focus on the "dual containment" of Iraq and Iran in the 1990's and certainly corresponded to Israel's longstanding desire to develop strong relations with non-Arab states on the periphery of the Arab world. But the most important driver here was the Kemalist elite's changed view of the value of the Israeli tie both domestically and in foreign policy. In the 1990s, the Turkish government also used the Israeli relationship to try to bolster its position with Congress to prevent the passage of resolutions on the Armenian Genocide.

---

*The coming to power of the AKP in the elections of 2002 changed the direction of this nascent triangular relationship, but not 180 degrees.*

---

The coming to power of the AKP in the elections of 2002 changed the direction of this nascent triangular relationship, but not 180 degrees. The

AKP approach to foreign policy (and it was free to pursue its approach, as it legislated a much reduced role for the military in foreign policy) is in many ways similar to that of Turgut Özal. It enthusiastically adopted Özal's export-led growth strategy and his openness to engagement in the Middle East. The AKP, contrary to its predecessors, chose to embrace the Kurdish Regional Government in Iraq, both as an important market for Turkish business and as part of its new thinking on how to deal with the domestic Kurdish issue. The "zero problems" policy toward neighbors signaled a new Turkish engagement in regional issues—better relations with Syria, Greece, and Armenia, engagement with Iran, and efforts to mediate a number of regional disputes. At the outset, this policy included maintaining very open and public relations with Israel. High-level visits were exchanged. Military purchases from each other continued. Economic relations grew. AKP leaders were at times critical of Israel's policy toward the Palestinians, but Prime Minister Bülent Ecevit had been at least as critical in the years before the AKP came to power. Most notably, the AKP government tried to facilitate Syrian-Israeli negotiations.

But, in the long run, the relationship built up between Turkey and Israel in the 1990s could not be sustained given the domestic political changes in Turkey (and, to some extent, in Israel, as will be discussed below). The Kemalist elite shared the Israeli view of Islamist politics as a threat, both regionally and domestically. The AKP did not share that view. Thus, Ankara and Jerusalem parted company on such important issues as how to deal with Iran, the victory of Hamas in the Palestinian elections of 2006, and Israel's use of military force in Lebanon in 2006 and Gaza in 2008-09. The more general democratization of Turkish foreign policy, with the reduction in the military's constitutional role in making it, meant that public opinion would play a greater role in its formation. Israeli policy in the second half of the 2000s led to very negative public opinion reactions in Turkey, which were then reflected in both the atmospherics of the relationship (e.g., Prime Minister Erdoğan's walk-out at Davos in 2009) and in its substance. The 2010 Turkish aid flotilla incident was the culmination of this process of distancing. The democratic and Islamist shifts in Turkish domestic politics have also complicated relations with the United States, though not nearly to the degree as is the case with Israel. As mentioned above, the Turkish parliament voted not to allow American troops access to Turkey during the 2003 Iraq War. This cannot be attributed to the AKP's Islamist orientation. Prime Minister Erdoğan supported the American request and most of his party, no doubt reluctantly, backed him. The Kemalist opposition torpedoed the resolution to embarrass the new AKP government, among other reasons. But it is clear evidence that more democratic politics in regional states makes it more difficult for them to support controversial

*The most important domestic political trend in post–Cold War Israel has been the strengthening of the Israeli right.*

American policies. The AKP's different disposition toward Islamist politics in general means that it has not joined American efforts to isolate Iran, though one can argue that Ankara's engagement with Tehran has the same end as America's policy of pressure. Anti-Americanism runs very high in Turkish public opinion now, according to the polls. Despite that, the AKP government has worked to maintain good relations with the United States for all sorts of reasons.

## Domestic Politics and Israeli Views of Turkey and the United States

The most important domestic political trend in post–Cold War Israel has been the strengthening of the Israeli right. That process did not begin in the 1990s, of course. Likud formed its first government in 1977. But, particularly since the 1990s, the steady movement of the center of Israeli politics to the right and the collapse of the Labor Party has complicated Israel's relations with both the United States (though not greatly) and Turkey (much more). On the American front, the rightward trend complicates relations on peace process issues. As indicated above, the changed global structure and the strength of pro-Israeli forces in American domestic politics seem to have reduced the salience of peace process issues for American presidents (despite the time they spend on it and their verbal support for progress). More rightist Israeli governments have more surface disputes with the United States, on issues like settlements, but those disputes do not escalate to crises. American presidents do not press the issue (George W. Bush); press the issue up to a point, but no further (Bill Clinton); or press the issue and then back down (Barack Obama). At some point, the rightward shift in Israeli politics might lead to a serious confrontation with the United States, but that has not happened yet.

The rightward trend is more important in Israeli-Turkish relations. It is no accident, as the Marxists like to say, that Turkey felt most comfortable in pursuing an openly cooperative relationship with Israel during the 1990s, when the peace process was in full flower. It is unlikely that the military had much concern for public opinion in its calculations of foreign policy making in the 1990s, but the peace process made it easier for elected Turkish governments of the 1990s to follow the army's lead. The AKP would have undoubtedly put more distance into the relationship even with a left-leaning Israeli government, but the rightward trend that was particularly strong in the 2000s widened the gap between Jerusalem and Ankara, and thus accelerated the decline of the bilateral relationship. One can hardly imagine the unfortunate, televised stunt of the Israeli deputy foreign minister humiliating the Turkish ambassador occurring if someone more centrist than Avigdor Lieberman were Israel's foreign minister.

## Conclusion: Lessons Learned from the Winter of Arab Discontent

The end of the Cold War was an important inflection point in American relations with both Israel and Turkey. The strongly constraining force of bipolarity helped to limit the influence of domestic politics on the U.S. bilateral relationship with both countries. With that constraint removed, domestic political factors have played a much larger role in each side of the strategic triangle. They have cemented American-Israeli relations even in the absence of a compelling strategic rationale. They drove Turkey closer to Israel in the 1990s and further away from Israel in the 2000s. They complicated American-Turkish strategic ties.

This conclusion raises the stakes of the current domestic political upheavals in the Arab world. Although we do not know how the politics of any of the Arab countries affected by these events will shake out, we can assume that more democratic politics in these countries will complicate their relations with both the United States and with Israel. The Turkish case indicates that a more democratic and Islamist government does not necessarily mean a complete break with the United States, on the model of revolutionary Iran, but it does mean more distance in the relationship and more difficulties in strategic cooperation. The Turkish case also indicates that a more democratic and Islamist government means a more difficult relationship with Israel, even if it does not mean open conflict and the rupturing of diplomatic relations. Although examination of Turkey does not support the direst forecasts of what the winter of Arab discontent might mean for the United States, it certainly suggests that relations between Washington and newly democratizing Arab states will be more stressful than with their authoritarian predecessors.

2

# Reshuffling the Cards: Turkey, Israel, and the United States in the Middle East

*Soli Özel, Istanbul Kadir Has University*

Whether they are to be considered revolts or revolutions, the popular uprisings in the Arab world drastically changed the strategic environment of the Middle East. As one Israeli author observed, all the assumptions for that country's strategic calculations had been destroyed in the course of a few weeks, particularly because of the developments in Egypt. Lately, the violent, protracted, and perhaps inevitable collapse of the Syrian regime, too, is causing growing concerns in Israel as in the rest of the region and beyond.

Similarly, the assumptions of the Turkish government for the conceptualization and conduct of its foreign policy were swept away by the unexpected and tumultuous developments in Turkey's neighborhood. A Turkish foreign policy based on engagement with existing regimes to create a zone of co-prosperity while increasing Turkey's visibility and appeal in surrounding societies lost its bearings. Most notably in Syria, the limits of Turkey's policy became obvious and led to a shift in Ankara's emphases and discourse.

For U.S. policymakers, the revolts in the Arab world also forced them to revisit and reexamine the long-latent tension between their focus on security/stability and their desire to adhere to their country's proclaimed values. As President Barack Obama said in his speech on May 19, 2011 about the Middle East, "We must acknowledge that a strategy based solely upon the narrow pursuit of these interests will not fill an empty stomach or allow someone to speak their mind . . . . We have a stake not just in the stability of nations, but in the self-determination of individuals. The status quo is not sustainable . . . . We support a set of universal rights."

The upgrading of principle over strategic interests meant that the United States would have a lot less influence over developments on the ground. For, by definition, peoples that enjoy full sovereignty will pursue their national interest irrespective of the strategic imperatives or demands of a third party, even if it is a close ally. In fact, the military-dominated transitional government of Egypt immediately began to veer away from former President Hosni Mubarak's line and gave signs of reconciliation with Iran. Furthermore, post-Mubarak Egypt took the lead in brokering a deal between rival Palestinian factions, partially opened the Rafah gateway to Gaza, hardened its stance vis-à-vis Israel, and began its comeback as the key Arab player in the region.

Many commentators who analyze President Obama's foreign policy have seen a move toward retrenchment and a more frugal use of America's declining resources. The logical corollary to such an analysis is the need for the United States to work with, and rely more heavily on, regional allies that will naturally have more say in the partnership. Washington's closest ally in the Gulf, Saudi Arabia, seemed infuriated by this apparent supremacy of principle over purpose and began to devise its own policy to deal with the troubles in its immediate vicinity. Riyadh defied an equivocating United States in Bahrain by taking a very hard-line position there. In short, the certainties of previous years, indeed decades, no longer obtain in this critical region and the new power balances will take a while to take shape.

Such a drastic transformation of a region that previously seemed outwardly lethargic also brought forth many questions concerning the nature of its future order. Indeed, some even questioned the sustainability of the political geography of the region that was, after all, shaped by imperial powers. The political division of the region did not quite correspond to its social and economic realities and was never thoroughly internalized by any of the peoples living there either.

Before the Arab world underwent these convulsions, one of the most stable relations of the region—between two of the region's non-Arab states, Turkey and Israel—had been deteriorating steadily since Israel's ill-fated Gaza War in 2008-09. Anti-Israeli rhetoric reached new heights on the Turkish side, particularly after the deadly and (for the Turks as well as the UN Human Rights Council) illegal attack by the Israeli military on a Turkish ship in May 2010. The *Mavi Marmara* was part of an international civilian flotilla taking aid material to Gaza to break the Israeli blockade. Nine Turks, one of whom was a Turkish American, lost their lives during the raid. A further escalation of the crisis was imminent when Israel wanted to keep the passengers in custody; that escalation was only averted through American intervention.

Since then, in Turkey, the ruling AKP has used every occasion to attack Israel. For its part, Israel's Knesset recently moved to change its stance on the alleged genocide of Ottoman Armenians, clearly an act of hostility as far as the Turks are concerned. Currently the two countries do not have serving ambassadors in one another's capital, although diplomatic relations have not been severed.

During Turkey's 2011 parliamentary elections campaign, the ruling party continued its Israel bashing, and *Mavi Marmara's* participation in a second flotilla in July 2011 seemed very likely, though it was prevented by the Ankara government at the last minute. Israeli newspapers reported that the Netanyahu government took a decision not to respond to attacks coming from Turkey lest such responses serve the interests of the AKP. In the wake of the elections of June 12, 2011, though, things began to move rapidly in a different direction. Twice, attempts to reconcile the two countries' positions on the *Mavi Marmara* incident have been aborted. (Turkey demands an official apology and compensation for the victims' families and deems the Israeli blockade of Gaza, and therefore the raid on the ship in international waters, illegal. The Israelis appear ready to pay compensation, but are unwilling to apologize and are ready only to extend their regret.) The Palmer Commission established by the UN Secretary General is supposed to clarify these matters, but the publication of its report has already been delayed several times.

This recent shift toward a more conciliatory approach by both parties is a function of the historic transformations in the Middle East. Ultimately, therefore, in terms of the relations between Israel and Turkey, and both countries' ties to the United States, the Arab revolts have had the effect of altering the terms of the debate and the position of the parties. The shock waves of the Arab revolts reinforced the structural/strategic necessity of cooperation between Turkey and Israel. Just a week before the end of the electoral campaign, the Turkish foreign minister, Ahmet Davutoğlu, who had been unyieldingly hard-line in his criticism of Israel, gave the first sign that continuing the mutually harsh rhetoric and the absence of dialogue have outlived their usefulness. The foreign minister urged the organizers of a second flotilla to halt their

*Recent shifts toward a more conciliatory approach by Turkey and Israel are a function of the Arab Spring uprisings in the Middle East.*

plans. In the wake of the Turkish elections, the İnsan Hak ve Hürriyetleri ve İnsannsani Yardım Vakfı/Humanitarian Relief Foundation (IHH), the NGO that owns *Mavi Marmara,* announced that, due to continuing "repair work," the ship could not join the second flotilla. On the Israeli side, the veteran Israeli journalist Zvi Bar'el of *Haaretz* noted the Turkish reversal and argued, "The Middle Eastern kaleidoscope has once again made a 180-degree turn, revealing a new picture. Prime Minister Benjamin Netanyahu's letter to Turkish Prime Minister Recep Tayyip Erdoğan congratulating him for his party's sweeping victory in the elections is only one aspect."[1]

The United States, too, has an interest in the amelioration of the relations between Israel and Turkey. Washington should have little patience for such tension between its two difficult regional partners. Bad relations between Turkey and Israel have spillover effects in a U.S. Congress that tries to penalize Ankara for its stance. Such moves have the potential to harm Turkish-American relations and, by extension, America's regional policy. At a time when Washington coordinates policy with Ankara on Syria, when the two sides cooperate on Iraq and Afghanistan, this is a condition that neither government should welcome.

It is necessary to conclude this introduction by noting the irony that Turkish-Israeli bilateral trade has steadily increased since the Gaza War and that there are on average three flights a day between Istanbul and Tel Aviv. According to a news report by *Hürriyet Daily News* on May 30, 2011, trade between Turkey and Israel increased by 25 percent between 2009 and 2010 and by 40 percent in the first quarter of 2011, compared to the same period a year earlier.

1. Zvi Bar'el, "Apologizing to Turkey is in Israel's interest," *Haaretz,* June 26, 2011. http://www.haaretz.com/print-edition/opinion/apologizing-to-turkey-is-in-israel-s-interest-1.369634.

It is safe to say, in light of these developments, that Turkish-Israeli relations will enter a new era. They will have to be redefined in view of the changing regional and global strategic realities. Israeli authorities evidently recognized how the current standoff with Turkey runs counter to their interests. As Anshel Pfeffer wrote in *Haaretz*, "Israel can take out one insurance policy to protect itself from the effects of the Arab revolution—a sharp and swift improvement in relations with Ankara . . . . The prolonged estrangement since Operation Cast Lead, which worsened with what happened on the *Mavi Marmara* and that flotilla to Gaza, is now hurting Israel far more than Turkey."[2]

The deepening of economic relations, the growing isolation of Israel in the international system, as well as its slow-paced but visible estrangement from the American administration, partially explain the Israeli shift. Turkey's need to rid itself of the Israeli obstacle in its relations with the United States as well as the pragmatic uses of having an open dialogue with Israel for Turkey's wider foreign policy ambitions help reinforce Ankara's inclination to patch up the relations. As in previous periods, the shape the relations will take should reflect the strategic framework of the period and the ranking order of the strategic players in this framework.

## The Historical Background: A Consistently Checkered History

Turkish-Israeli and Turkish-American relations moved on separate tracks during the Cold War. Turkey's shifting position vis-à-vis the Jewish state had to do with its concerns about Soviet influence in the Middle East and the desire to ingratiate itself to its future major ally, the United States. Turkey first voted against the creation of a Jewish and an Arab state in Palestine in 1947, but then recognized Israel (the first Muslim country to do so) in March 1949, and established diplomatic relations with it in 1950. This was an ambivalent relationship from the outset. The Turkish public's sensitivity for the plight of the Palestinians and the Turkish state's desire not to alienate the Arab states were always in the back of the Turkish diplomatic mind. Therefore, relations with Israel were kept at a distance.

According to Israeli scholar Ofra Bengio, the ambivalence of Turkey's attitude toward Israel was crystallized in the positions Turkey took during

---

2. Anshel Pfeffer, "Erdoğan, the Strongest Leader in the Middle East," *Haaretz*, June 16, 2010. http://www.haaretz.com/print-edition/opinion/erdogan-the-strongest-leader-in-the-mideast-1.367992.

three of Israel's post-independence wars. Turkey remained militarily neutral, but withstood Arab pressure to sever its relations with the Jewish state. Following the Suez War, Ankara reduced its representation to the *chargé d'affaires* level, citing Israeli occupation of the Sinai Peninsula, and did not upgrade it after the Israeli Defense Forces withdrew. During the crisis of 1967, Turkey refused to contribute to the efforts to reopen the Gulf of Aqaba to Israeli shipping and closed the Incirlik Air Base to American military forces.[3] In 1973, Turkey again denied the use of Incirlik to the United States. There are also reports that Ankara allowed the use of its airspace to Soviet cargo planes that were taking ammunition to Egypt during the war.

Ambivalence was not the only attribute that defined these relations. They were also uneven. Israel's desire to be recognized in the region and its peripheral alliance strategy made Turkey's friendship very valuable. Turkey, on the other hand, did not wish to be intimate with Israel. When the two countries came closer, for Ankara this was usually the result of expediency, as in the wake of the Iraqi coup of 1958. Even then, there was no public display of cooperation or closeness and the Israeli prime minister, David Ben Gurion, could only visit Turkey in secret in 1958. In fact, in 1966, Turkey abruptly cancelled intelligence cooperation with Israel, but it never did break diplomatic relations with Tel Aviv, even when it was actively trying to recruit Arab states to support its position on Cyprus.

Turkey's moves to get closer to the Arab world continued with the recognition of the PLO as the sole and legitimate representative of the Palestinians and its vote in favor of the UN resolution that equated Zionism with racism. The bottom was hit when, in the wake of Israel's declaration in 1980 that "united Jerusalem" was its capital, Ankara brought its representation down to the second-secretary level and, despite secret intelligence and military cooperation, diplomatic relations remained publicly cool till after the first Gulf War.

## After the Berlin Wall Fell

The drastic changes that marked the end of the Cold War dramatically altered the strategic calculus of the Western security system. Global developments in the context of post–September 11 developments have

3. Ofra Bengio, *Turkiye-Israil: Hayalet Ittifaktan Stratejik Isbirligine*, (Istanbul: Erguvan Yayinevi, 2009), pp.115-117.

further transformed the security perceptions of the key actors in the international arena. Thus, the radical change in the source and nature of threats gave way to Turkey's search for a new role, strategy, and set of policies, particularly toward its neighborhood. In the second decade of the post–Cold War era, in the wake of the September 11 attacks and the American misadventure in Iraq, Turkey's regional strategic profile would rise considerably, and its foreign policy would carve for itself a zone of autonomous action.

Turkey had been a staunch ally of the United States and member of NATO throughout the Cold War era. Hence, from the beginning, Turkish-American relations were defined mainly, if not exclusively, along the security dimension. Throughout the Cold War, the military aspect always remained the core of the relationship. As a result, the strongest institutional link that existed between the two countries was the military one. In time, the Pentagon and the Turkish General Staff turned into the most reliable and trusted points of contact for each other. As such, they were able to maintain relatively stable links and a healthy respect for each other even in times of serious difficulties in bilateral relations between the two countries.

Be that as it may at the security level, relations became more complicated at the end of the Cold War. With the end of the bipolar era and the absence of the Soviet threat, Turkey's geostrategic importance at first came under increasing scrutiny. The interests of the two partners diverged, as was to be expected between a global and a regional power in the absence of a well-defined common threat. Operations "Desert Shield" and "Desert Storm," and the subsequent "Operation Provide Comfort" in Iraq made Turkey uncomfortable. Iraq's meaning for Americans and the Turks was altogether different, and the tensions that would fully come to surface on the eve of the 2003 Iraq War were there throughout the 1990s. Still, both the Iraq crisis/war and the subsequent dissolution of Yugoslavia, along with the collapse of the Soviet Union, recalibrated Turkey's strategic importance. The opening of the vast, energy-rich Caucasus and Central Asia, and the creation of newly independent states out of the ex-Soviet world helped raise Turkey's profile, and the first discussions about Turkey serving as a "model" surfaced during this "genesis" period.

Although committed to the transatlantic alliance, Turkey for some time has also displayed the symptoms of an "alliance-security dilemma." Such alliance-security dilemmas are exacerbated by fear of abandonment or isolation. Since the end of the Cold War, Turkey periodically suffered from such fears. It felt unsure of its place in the Western alliance and the institutions, such as NATO, not to mention the European Union. The post–Iraq War transatlantic rift and U.S. unilateralism, particularly in Iraq while George W. Bush was the U.S. President, had also heightened Turkish anxiety regarding U.S. intentions.

In the early 1990s, a deficit of trust emerged on the part of Turkey, even if that was not articulated, concerning the ultimate intentions of the United States vis-à-vis the Kurds of Iraq. These were somewhat dissipated when the United States delivered the leader of the PKK, Abdullah Öcalan, who was a guest at the Greek Embassy in Nairobi, to a Turkish military team in Kenya in 1999. In some sense the delivery of Öcalan was the culmination of developments in American foreign policy, a brainchild of the late diplomat Richard Holbrooke, that placed Turkey near the center of a new strategic conceptualization in the Greater Middle East. In short, this new perspective on Turkey, articulated in different times with fairly similar emphases by Presidents Clinton, George W. Bush, and Obama, valued the country as much for what it was as for where it was.

In Holbrooke's terminology, Turkey was the frontline state of the post–Cold War era. Since there was no imminent threat of war, its defining characteristics elevated Turkey to such a central role. From Morocco to Afghanistan, a vast region was defined by authoritarianism, resistance to globalization (both economically and politically), corruption, youth bulges, and increasingly by its proclivity to generate violent Islamist radicalism. Almost at the center of that area, close to the energy resources of the Caspian Basin as well as the Gulf, Turkey stood as a capitalist, secular, pluralist (if not yet totally democratic) Muslim country that was a member of the Atlantic Alliance. The American efforts to open the path for Turkey's EU accession ought to be seen in the context of Washington's desire to see Ankara fully integrated in the transatlantic system as a *bona fide* democratic country. In view of Turkey's domestic developments during the first decade of the post–Cold War era, this latter attribute meant the integration of the Islamist movement fully into the political system and a resolution of Turkey's Kurdish problem by an extension of citizenship rights. President Clinton, who said at the Turkish Grand National Assembly in 1999 that the 21st century would be largely shaped by decisions that Turkey took, was the first president to articulate this thinking. This approach culminated in President Obama's declaration that the United States and Turkey were in a "model partnership" during his visit (the first official bilateral visit of his presidency) to Ankara in April 2009.

The trouble with this scheme was the resistance to such democratizing change in Turkey's political system that was sustained from within its power structure. Indeed, by substituting the threat of separatist Kurdish terrorism and a loosely defined Islamist regression, the military-bureaucratic elites of Turkey and their civilian allies resisted all attempts to liberalize/democratize the political system. During that period, all issues on the country's agenda were treated as security issues, and therefore the political space for treating the country's ills had narrowed considerably. The miserable performance of second-rate politicians and the general instability of the country's politics made the 1990s a lost decade of political decay and boom and bust economic cycles. At the same time, though, the strengthening signs of a new Turkey and corresponding new politics were surfacing rapidly.

During the 1990s, Turkey felt increasingly isolated from its allies because of their criticism of the way the military and the security apparatus were carrying out counter-insurgency operations against suspected members and supporters of the then-separatist organization, the PKK. (This campaign included undertaking extra-judicial executions of suspects.) Feeling shunned by their allies, unable to get the kind of intelligence and material they needed to conduct the counterinsurgency, and surrounded by hostile neighbors, Turkish security officials looked intently for a way to break out of their impasse.

## Turkish-Israeli Alignment: The Golden Age

When the strategic love affair between Israel and Turkey was made public in March 1996, Turkey had conflictual relations with six out of its nine neighbors. Earlier in the year, Turkey and Greece came very close to war over the uninhabited twin islets of Imia/Kardak in the Aegean. Syria was hosting Turkey's public enemy number one, Abdullah Öcalan, the leader of the separatist PKK, and allowing the PKK's forces to train in the Bekaa Valley.

The attempt by Greek Cypriots to buy S-300 missiles from Russia in 1997-98 provoked a strong and belligerent reaction from the Turkish military. Iran was accused of both aiding the PKK when it served its purposes and of complicity in terrorist activities inside Turkey. The PKK itself used the Kandil Mountains in northern Iraq to stage its terrorist attacks against Turkey. Last but not least, Turkey had no diplomatic relations with Armenia.

Domestically, the military's grip over civilian politics increased considerably in the wake of President Turgut Özal's untimely death in 1993. The succession of ineffectual, mostly corrupt, and incompetent coalition governments kept on postponing necessary economic, political, and administrative reforms. As the establishment parties steadily lost their grip on a disenchanted electorate, the Islamists gained ground and, in December 1995, came out of the general elections as the largest party in the country.

As I pointed out earlier, within its alliance system Turkey was nearly a pariah state. The country was unable to get technological and material support or buy the required weapons from its allies in its fight against terrorism because of its egregious human rights violations, particularly in the southeast of the country where most of its Kurdish citizens lived. In the United States, two powerful lobbies in Congress constantly battered Turkey. Both the Greek and Armenian lobbies at the time were venomous in their approach to all matters Turkish.

The "strategic alignment" with Israel occurred under such circumstances. It was masterminded by the military and aimed at breaking Turkey's isolation internationally in its fight against the PKK, thus sending a strong message to its hostile neighbors and reminding the traditionally Israel-averse Islamists who the master was. As Turkish analyst Gencer Özcan has summed it up:

> Alignment with Israel was devised to meet a number of strategic requirements . . . . In the nineties Turkey's regional outlook in the Middle East was overwhelmed by its struggle with the Kurdish separatist movement that used Northern Iraq as a rear base and received support from Syria and Iran. Therefore, the regionalization of Kurdish separatism compelled Ankara to formulate an assertive policy for which Israel appeared to be a suitable partner. Furthermore, Israeli readiness to respond to Turkey's procurement of military supplies served as another element in the making of the alignment. Intelligence sharing and cooperation on other security related issues were key elements of the rapprochement and therefore major actors who played a key role in the making of the alignment came from the security establishments.[4]

---

4. Gencer Özcan, "Turkish-Israeli Relations in Crisis: How to Cut the Gordian Knot?" draft paper presented at *The Impact of Turkey-Israel Relations on EU Policies in the Mediterranean*, Barcelona, April 12, 2011, quoted with permission of the author.

The agreements between Israel and Turkey at first exacerbated the Arabs' ingrained suspicions of Ankara and its intentions. However, the success of Turkish diplomacy in convincing the Arab states that this alignment was not meant against them, and the usefulness of Turkey's open channels to Israel for all the other parties, soon balanced the initial reaction. Within three years, Turkey's relations with Greece had ameliorated, as did the ones with Iran. The Turkish military gained confidence and ground in its fight against the PKK, with the help of intelligence, technology, and materiel from Israel. Ankara put Syria on notice and forced Damascus to break with Öcalan. Ankara also received precious support from the Israeli lobby in the United States to stave off "genocide" resolutions in the U.S. Congress and developed a close relation with some Jewish organizations.

Israel finally had what it desired since its foundation: open and publically close relations with Turkey. It also benefited economically from these relations; Israeli citizens felt welcomed in Istanbul or Antalya. Militarily, the Israeli Air Force greatly appreciated the opportunity to train in the skies over the vast Konya Valley. These relations made sense strategically, and both parties were content to deepen them. But from the Turkish perspective, there was a catch. The legitimacy of these intimate relations depended on the existence of a viable and credible Arab-Israeli peace process. In other words, what made this alignment possible was the existence of the Oslo process. The Turkish public was historically pro-Palestinian and strongly favored an independent Palestinian state. Therefore, when the relations between Israel and the Palestinians deteriorated in the wake of the Second Intifada and there was no longer a peace process to speak of, the moral basis of the alignment eroded considerably.

In the meantime, Turkey changed. The introverted, hard-core militarist Turkey gradually gave way to a Turkey that was opening up and preparing itself for EU membership. Its economy expanded. Long-postponed administrative and political reforms began to be enacted, at first gradually, by old-school politicians thanks to the EU accession process. Under the rule of a new political party, the AKP, which had its roots in the traditionally anti-Western Islamist movement, the process rapidly progressed. A major power shift began to take place domestically as well. The military's hold over Turkey's politics was finally on the wane. New elites began to replace the old ones, economically, socially, and politically. Turkey's periphery, historically excluded from determining the political space, moved into the center.

Soon the shocks in the international system and in the region would change Turkey's environment and the setting of its relations with Israel radically.

## September 11 and the Iraq War

The period between al-Qaeda's attacks against the United States on September 11, 2001, and the still-unfolding Arab revolts of 2010-11, brought dramatic changes to the international system and the Middle Eastern regional order. The cumulative effect of America's wars against Afghanistan and Iraq was a diminution of American power and prestige around the world. The financial burdens of the two wars, no less than their political damage, led the United States to begin a policy of gradual retrenchment. The war against Iraq, in particular, disrupted the fragile balances of the Middle Eastern regional system. The Arab state system collapsed under the weight of its fissures, its deepening legitimacy crisis, and its inability to deal with the need for change. To boot, the American war against Iraq had the unintended consequence of raising Iran's profile and making it not only the predominant regional power in the Persian Gulf, but also an Eastern Mediterranean power because of its organic links to Hizbollah in Lebanon.

Contrary to the expectations of the architects of the Iraq War, Israel did not come out as a winner from the war either. True, the major (if ineffectual and inconsequential) headache that Saddam's Iraq had been, was forced from the regional stage. But the increasing Iranian influence exacerbated Israeli apprehensions and anxieties about the Islamic Republic, which the Israelis had been predicting for the previous two decades would become a nuclear power in the next two years. Far more importantly though, the Iraq War, once the shortcomings of the American expedition became obvious, had a more profound impact that was not immediately visible.

In my judgment, the Iraq War inadvertently terminated the framework of the Nixon Doctrine that, since 1969 (an outcome of the 1967 Arab-Israeli war) incrementally gave Israel more of a central role in America's regional policy. Israeli military might, the shift in Egypt's strategic leanings, and the Iranian Revolution all enhanced Israel's status and led its politicians to enact with impunity both their imperial designs (the case of Lebanon) and their expansionist settlement policies. Aside from a valiant attempt by George H. W. Bush at the end of the Cold War, right after

Desert Storm, the American administrations did not push Israel particularly hard toward peace. President Clinton's last-hour efforts floundered, both because of the Palestinian leadership's ineptitude and the assumptions and limitations of American policymakers.

In the aftermath of the Iraq War, this strategic framework that overly privileged Israel should be less compelling. We can see manifestations of this sea change in the continuing tensions between Tel Aviv and Washington, and in the declarations of American officials, military and civilian alike. Furthermore, the intellectual debate in the United States questioning the policy toward Israel has intensified. Israel's influence in American domestic politics can only hold this barrage for a while longer, but not for too long.

Contrary to its impact on Israel, both September 11 and the Iraq War ultimately benefited Turkey. If September 11 gave the world a taste of the jihadist dystopia, Turkey certainly stood as an antidote and an antithesis to it. Turkey's historically shaped characteristics provided an example to the world in general that another type of politics was possible than either the stagnant Arab Middle Eastern one or the messianic Iranian one or the violence-worshipping jihadism. Soon the ascent to power of the AKP, a party with an Islamist pedigree, would make the Turkish experiment even more of a shining example.

Many of the decision makers in the Turkish state and among the public were vehemently opposed to the Iraq War. Although the Turkish government negotiated with the United States to allow the deployment of American troops on its territory so that a northern front could be opened, the Parliament ultimately rejected the government's decree. Turkish-American relations were thus severely bruised. This refusal, and the subsequent internment of Turkish special operations soldiers by American troops in the town of Suleimanieh in northern Iraq on July 4, 2003, were the flash points of the deterioration in relations.

The truth is, though, that Iraq, since the invasion of Kuwait and Operation Desert Storm, was already a source of tension in bilateral relations. It crystallized the divergence of views between Turkey and the United States, or between the interests of an aspiring regional power and the global power, in the post–Cold War setting. It exacerbated on the Turkish side fears of an independent Kurdistan to the south of its border and raised suspicions of U.S. connivance in that project.

Despite warmer relations in the second half of the 1990s, close cooperation to finalize the construction of the Baku–Tbilisi–Ceyhan pipeline that turned Turkey into an energy transport route, and the celebration of a vaguely defined "special partnership," the two sides never really sorted out their potential disagreements. In the absence of a mutually agreed-upon framework for moving these relations forward, accidents could and ultimately did happen. As far as Turkey was concerned, the Iraq adventure produced all the results that Ankara warned Washington about. Turkey also had to face and deal with the mostly negative consequences of this expedition. In order to do so Ankara took many initiatives even before the war began.

After the war, Ankara, whose offer to send troops to Iraq was turned down by the Iraqi government because of Kurdish resistance to such a move, was unresponsive to American demands that it downgrade its relations with Iran, a member of the "axis of evil," and Syria. On the other hand, Turkish cooperation with the United States in Iraq continued despite great dissatisfaction with the level and quality of U.S. help in fighting the PKK. In the meantime, as the full scale of the political failures of the American side in Iraq became apparent, Turkish efforts to integrate the Sunnis into the political process, Ankara's ability to speak with all the Arab Iraqi parties, and its constructive initiatives for mediation gained the genuine appreciation of all concerned parties.

In fact, Turkish foreign policy became ever more active, and the domestic developments favoring civilianization and democratization of the polity gradually loosened the grip the Turkish military had on devising the proper policy toward Iraq and its Kurds in particular. In view of the shifts in Turkish policy vis-à-vis Iraqi Kurdistan, the second Bush administration, after the appointment of Robert Gates as secretary of defense, changed America's approach toward Turkey. The most important sign of this change came at the conclusion of the critical meeting between President Bush and Prime Minister Erdoğan in Washington on November 5, 2007. The president then called "the PKK an enemy of Iraq, Turkey, and the United States," and gave the green light for providing actionable intelligence to the Turkish military. Thereupon, Turkish policy toward Iraqi Kurdistan began to change dramatically, intensifying economic integration and political cooperation with the Kurdish Regional Government.

When it came to power, the AKP simultaneously pursued EU accession and engagement with its neighboring regions. Although the party did not invent this policy of rapprochement, it certainly deepened it. Turkey's interest and involvement in the region increased considerably.

Not only did the credibility of the country hit new heights because of the Parliament's refusal to allow the deployment of American troops to open a northern front against Iraq, but its political scene endeared it to the publics in the Middle East.

No longer considered a threat by its neighbors, the Turkey that relied heavily on its hard power, that shunned the Middle East, where the military called all the important shots, segued into a Turkey that was capable of deploying its soft power. It set an example of a country that could integrate its Islamists into the political system, continue in its democratic practices, and show impressive economic growth. Arab citizens discovered Turkey in ever growing numbers, just as Turkish TV series started to dominate prime-time airwaves throughout the region. As Turkey's policy toward its neighbors gradually became less confrontational, the benefits of the Israeli alignment became relatively less impressive than before. In the meantime, the architect of that alignment on the Turkish side, the military, was fast losing political ground as a result of intensive civilianization and further democratization of the polity, as well as indictments against its members for alleged coup plots and other illicit activities. Therefore, the Turkish-Israeli relationship needed new columns to stand on.

In its foreign policy, the AKP committed itself to the principle of "zero problems" with the neighbors, moved in to fill the vacuum created by the United States, and volunteered its good offices for mediation in the long-standing conflicts of the region, particularly those that concerned Israel.

The problem was that the two countries had diverging visions for the Middle East, and their policy preferences and approaches were increasingly irreconcilable. Turkey increasingly sees itself as a regional power and seeks to be America's main partner in the region. Under the rubric of "model partnership," Ankara believes that it has a chance to forge such a relationship that will inevitably come at the expense of Israel's most-favored and protected status.

Turkey wishes to have a Middle East order that is based on economic integration, political stability, and peace. Achieving peace is seen as the precondition of political stability, and economic integration was expected to consolidate that stability. As Gencer Özcan notes:

> Many observers branded the change as one of transformation from a national security state to a trading state. Reflecting Turkey's growing self-confidence, lifting visa requirements with many neighbors is also related with this transformation . . . . Now figures of incoming and outgoing

> tourists from and to the neighboring countries are in steady increase. Moreover, Arab markets are flooded with Turkish goods, while Turkish TV serials are becoming popular across the Middle East.[5]

Ankara believed Israel's current policies were blocking this path of regional integration. Whereas Israel imposed the siege of Gaza, Turkey believed it must be ended and a way must be found to engage Hamas in the political process.

In fact, engaging with non-state actors such as Hizbollah, the Muslim Brotherhood, and Iraqi groups around the region had also become a mainstay of Turkish foreign policy. Many of these sought "Turkish diplomats' good offices for the local crises they try to cope with and turned Ankara into a sort of diplomatic *Mecca*."[6] This may yet prove to be a choice that is likely to yield political and diplomatic benefits in the wake of the Arab revolts.

The centerpiece of Turkey's Middle East policy was Syria. The Turkish government gave cover to the Syrian regime at its most vulnerable, when former Prime Minister Rafik Hariri of Lebanon was murdered and Damascus was suspected of masterminding the deed. Turkey put great energy, despite U.S. objections, into brokering a Syrian-Israeli deal in 2008. The fury of Prime Minister Erdoğan in the wake of the Gaza War in part stemmed from the fact that the war killed an Israeli-Syrian agreement that the Turkish side believed was almost struck during Ehud Olmert's visit to Ankara days before Operation Cast Lead.

---

*Turkey, over the last decade, banked on the established regimes to pursue its active and engaged foreign policy. That order has now collapsed.*

---

Finally, not only does Turkey continue to engage Iran, despite criticism that Tehran uses these efforts to gain time for further nuclear enrichment, but also Ankara continues to raise Israel's nuclear arsenal on every platform. The decision of the 2010 Non-Proliferation Treaty (NPT) Review Conference that invited Israel to open its nuclear program to scrutiny

5. Özcan, op. cit.
6. Özcan, op. cit.

proved that Turkey's persistence on this matter paid off. The AKP government tried to engage Tehran in bilateral relations and improved trade and investment. It pursued a line that was different than its Western allies concerning Iran's nuclear program. It went so far as brokering a swap deal on nuclear fuel along with Brazil. Then Ankara voted against Iranian sanctions at the UN Security Council. That last move certainly irritated the Obama administration and subsequent developments suggest that the Turkish government has learned its lesson as well. In truth, Turkey's Iran policy is more complicated than meets the eye as Ankara is in competition with Tehran for influence in Syria, Lebanon, Gaza, and most importantly, Iraq. From that perspective, the visit to Iraq by Prime Minister Erdoğan in March 2011, when he visited, as a Sunni head of government, Najaf, prayed at Ali's shrine, and paid a visit to Ayatollah Ali Sistani, assumes critical importance.

In sum, Turkey and Israel saw their interests and policies diverge drastically in the decade between 2001 and 2011. Yet, despite the divergences and increasingly bellicose rhetoric that originated on both sides, relations were maintained. It is enough to look at some of these developments to dismiss the simplistic arguments that the problem in Turkish-Israeli relations stems from the AKP's past, ideology, and reflexive anti-Israeli stance. Not only did Ankara keep silent when Israeli jets violated Turkish airspace when they bombed Syrian nuclear facilities in 2007, but also Ankara, despite great pressure from the Palestinians, refused to veto Israel's admission to the Organization for Economic Co-operation and Development (OECD) only days before the *Mavi Marmara* calamity. Since the deadly raid against the *Mavi Marmara*, Turkey and Israel have kept high-level contacts, Turkey assisted Israel by sending two planes to extinguish the forest fire that broke out in Mount Carmel, and the Turkish Armed Forces kept receiving training for Heron Unmanned Aerial Vehicles and used them in northern Iraq. Last but not least, for the first time in Turkish history, Holocaust Day was commemorated in Istanbul with the participation of municipal and provincial authorities as well as a representative from the Turkish foreign ministry.

## Beyond Gaza and the *Mavi Marmara* in the Age of Arab Revolts

In my judgment, the flotilla tragedy was a consequence of the politics of miscalculation on both sides. I find the Israeli position legally untenable and politically inexcusable. Yet I do not believe the Israelis intended the matters to get out of hand. The Turkish government could have blocked the flotilla and chose not to do so because it wanted to generate domestic support for the upcoming referendum on constitutional amendments. Turkish authorities empathically argued after the incident that they had a deal with the Israeli authorities on how to prevent a confrontation, implying that Israel reneged on its promises. The fact that the Turkish undersecretary was in Washington and Foreign Minister Davutoğlu was on his way to Washington to meet with the Israeli Prime Minister Netanyahu, who had a scheduled appointment with Hillary Clinton, gives credence to this argument.

The tragic incident is also symptomatic of the power struggle between the two countries. As I have argued, Turkey wishes to be the preeminent regional power and Washington's main ally in the region. As an aspiring regional hegemon, it wants an end to the privileging of Israeli policies and positions by Washington since it sees the absence of peace as a great threat to regional stability. Similarly, I think there are those in Israel who would not wish to give Turkey the opportunity to establish itself as a more consequential player than Israel in the eyes of Washington.

The Arab revolts, as I suggested at the beginning of this essay, fundamentally altered the strategic environment and the parties' calculations. Turkey, over the last decade, banked on the established regimes to pursue its active and engaged foreign policy. That order has now collapsed. Nowhere is the failure of pursuing "constructive engagement" more evident than in Syria. But the AKP's and its kindred organizations' organic links to some opposition movements in the region will place Turkey in a comfortable position to adjust to the new political realities as well. Already Turkish foreign policy discourse refers to a "policy of conscience" and highlights the importance of democracy, human rights, and political participation. Gone are the days when friendly regimes like that of Sudan would be let off the hook on claims of genocide because "Muslims don't commit genocide," or when the harsh repression of the Iranian regime in the wake of the 2009 presidential elections would be passed over in deafening silence.

As for Israel, the inadvisability of having adversarial relations with Turkey, particularly as the strategic edifice of the past 30-plus years is collapsing, must be clear to many Israelis. Whether or not the two sides will be able to come up with the proper formula so that both can claim to have gotten what they wanted from the *Mavi Marmara* probe conducted by the

Palmer Commission remains to be seen. If that hurdle can be overcome though, the conditions of the Golden Age of the 1990s are not going to return. Israel and Turkey will have to redefine and rebuild their relations according to the new regional circumstances and realities.

*Israel and Turkey will have to redefine and rebuild their relations according to the new regional circumstances and realities.*

So far, the Obama administration has given every sign that it understands the importance of maintaining Turkish-Israeli relations on the right track. If it can help find the path for the process of reconstruction in these relations to start, it will also have served American regional and global interests well.

3

# The Israeli-Turkish Relationship

*Shlomo Brom, Institute for National Security Studies*

Since the inception of the State of Israel, the Israeli-Turkish relationship has followed a cyclical pattern with ups and downs following each other. The reason for that was mainly the tension between, on the one hand, a set of common interests and potential affinity based on some similarities between the two states, and on the other hand, another set of differing interests and potential hostility based on dissimilarities between the two states.

Both states are non-Arab nation-states in a Middle East that is mostly Arab, and therefore Arab nationalism and pan-Arabism were for them, to some extent, a common enemy. The two states were part of the Western Bloc during the Cold War era and still retain a strong relationship with the United States and Europe. Turkey is a formal member of NATO, has an association agreement with the European Union, and in recent years has engaged in negotiations toward joining the European Union as a full-fledged member. Israel has also a close alliance with the United States and extensive relations with Europe. Both have a strong segment of secular population. Israel and Turkey adopted a free-market economic system and were integrated into the global economy and the globalization process successfully. Finally, in both states the military/security establishment played a major historical role.

There have also been a number of important dissimilarities between them. The two states are nation-states, but Turkey is a Muslim state and

Israel is a Jewish state in a situation of hostile relations between Muslims and Jews as a result of the Arab-Israeli conflict. Secondly, Turkey is a large state with aspirations for an important regional and global position. Israel is a small state with more modest ambitions. While Israel has faced continuous Arab hostility, Turkey has had common interests and usually reasonably good relationships with most of the Arab states. Moreover, whereas Israel is an established democracy, Turkey has moved through periods of military rule, dysfunctional democracies, and a combination of both.

The relationship between the two states improved when the common interests derived from their similarities were strong and the differing interests based on their dissimilarities were weakened as a result of domestic, regional, and global developments; and the opposite happened when the situation was reversed.

## The Turkish-Israeli Spring of 1993-2003

The last period of good relations that lasted from 1993-2003 is a good example of the power of these parameters. In the domestic arena, right at the beginning of this period, Turkish Prime Minister Süleyman Demirel's party, a secular liberal party, won the elections. The Turkish military establishment still played a major role and had much influence on domestic and foreign policies. In Israel, Yitzhak Rabin's government, which was open to rapprochement with the Arab world, replaced Yitzhak Shamir's "status quo" government.

In the regional arena, from the point of view of the Turkish regime, the most significant security and foreign policy issue—also having important domestic policy implications—was the Kurdish insurgency led by the Kurdistan Workers Party (PKK). As a result, Turkey's relations with its Arab neighbors and Iran deteriorated. That included Hafez al-Asad's Syria, which gave refuge to the PKK and its leadership, and Saddam Hussein's Iraq, which did not stop the PKK from operating

---

*The U.S. invasions of Iraq and Afghanistan and the collapse of the peace process weakened U.S. power in the Middle East . . . .*

---

from northern Iraq. At the same time, Israel was engaged in active peace negotiations with its Arab neighbors, Arab-Israeli tensions were relaxed, and there was a clear improvement in the relationship between Israel and the Arab world.

Globally, the world order had changed. The Soviet Union and the Warsaw Pact collapsed. The United States was left as the only superpower. This change was very meaningful for Turkey because, on the one hand, it strengthened the Turkish interest in becoming more closely integrated with the West and NATO, thus being on the side of the winners. But on the other hand, it raised concerns that Turkey had lost its strategic importance for the West as a bulwark against the Soviet Union.

These changes created the environment for a rapid development of the Israeli-Turkish relationship. The common interests of cooperating in combating shared enemies—the radical Arab states and Iran—and in developing the two states' relationships with their Western allies were dominant. The similarities in character and values were emphasized, as the two states were non-Arab, secular, and democratic in a Middle East that was mostly Arab, authoritarian, and going through a wave of growing Islamization. On the other hand, the dissimilarities, and mainly the fact that the Turkish population is predominantly Muslim, played a smaller role because of the weakening tensions between the Arabs and Israel following the progress in the peace process.

Although the descriptions of a strategic alliance between the two states were a little bit exaggerated because there were still divergent interests and constraints that were a result of Turkey being a Muslim state, the two states succeeded in building a very close relationship. This can be described as the creation and strengthening of an axis of friendship based on close military, economic, and foreign policy cooperation in some areas.

A good relationship with a big and important Muslim state is proof that Israel is a legitimate entity in the Middle East and can be accepted by the Muslim world. Turkey could also serve as a bridge to, and an intermediary with, Arab and Muslim states. On the other hand, any worsening of the relations with Turkey would only increase the sense of isolation among Israelis.

Military cooperation with Turkey also provides Israel with many benefits. It is a good market for its defense industries. It can provide the Israeli armed forces (and mostly the Air Force) with vast training areas. The geographical location of Turkey makes it a valuable asset in the areas of intelligence and operational cooperation. Another benefit was the fact that some Arab states that had a hostile relationship with Israel had also to invest forces on the Turkish front at the expense of their military deployment closer to Israel.

Economically, the two states are complementary. While Israel provides innovation, hi-tech products, advanced farming products, and a sophisticated financial system, Turkey provides a huge market, economies of scale, and cheap labor. The two states are close geographically and transportation costs are low. It is not surprising that the better political and military relations enabled a surge in trade and tourism.[1]

## The Decline of Israeli-Turkish Relations

The decline in the Israeli-Turkish relationship after 2003 can be attributed to changes in these same three arenas. In the domestic arena, the Justice and Development Party (AKP), led by Recep Tayyip Erdoğan, rose to power. This government, which was then reelected in 2007 (and again in June 2011), took Turkey through sweeping political, economic, and social changes and reforms. The most important in this context were the reduction in the power of the military establishment and rapid economic growth, making Turkey a candidate for the title of the next rising Asian economic tiger. Although the AKP does not define itself as an Islamic party, it is to some extent an offshoot of previous Islamic parties that were banned from participation in elections. Elements of Islamic political thinking and patterns of behavior, and affinity with the Islamic world, are playing a role in the policies of the party, domestically and externally. That meant that Turkey became more sensitive to the friction between Israel and the Arabs and more attuned to the Arab perceptions and policies.

In the regional arena, the Israeli-Palestinian peace process reached a situation of almost clinical death. The U.S. invasions of Iraq and Afghanistan and the collapse of the peace process weakened substantially U.S. power in the Middle East and increased the friction between Arabs and Muslims, on the one hand, and the West—led by the United States—on the other. Turkey under Erdoğan and his foreign minister, Ahmet Davutoğlu, made a turn to a more Middle Eastern policy and adopted a policy of "strategic depth" and "zero problems with neighbors," which involved active

---

1. In 2008, the peak of the economic relations, exports to Turkey reached $1,610 million US, and imports reached $1,388 million US, according to the data of the Israeli Central Bureau of Statistics. That does not include exports by the defense industries. http://www.cbs.gov.il/reader/?MIval=cw_usr_view_Folder&ID=141

attempts to solve the conflicts and ameliorate the relations with its neighboring states, including Syria, Iran, and Iraq.

In the global arena, a change in the balance of forces has also been gradually taking place, a move from a unipolar world in which the United States is the only superpower to a more multipolar world. That meant that the Turkish relationship with the United States became less important and more conflictual.

As a result, the common Turkish-Israeli interests have been weakened and the affinity has been replaced by hostility. Bad management of the relationship influenced too much by emotional reactions did not help and created incidents that poured additional oil onto the fire.

## A More Balanced View of Turkey

There has been a tendency in Israel in recent years to look at the Middle East mostly through the prism of the conflict between, on the one hand, the so-called "radical/extreme/Islamist/Shiite" states and non-state actors, led by Iran, and on the other, the axis of the so-called "pragmatic" states, led by Egypt and Saudi Arabia. As a result, a common view in Israel looks at the change in Turkish positions vis-à-vis Israel as a result of a rapprochement between Turkey and the "radical" axis and actually a gradual joining by Turkey of this "axis of evil," attributing all that to the Islamic nature of its government.

This perception reflects, of course, a shallow understanding of Turkish interests and of the developments in the Turkish policies, which are much more nuanced, sophisticated, and complex. First, Turkey does not have only shared interests with Iran. On the one hand, the economic relationship with Iran and cooperation in dealing with the Kurds are important to Turkey, and it would not like to be in a situation in which another Muslim state is bullied or attacked militarily by the United States or Israel, with all the repercussions of such an attack. On the other hand, Turkey and Iran, as the two rising non-Arab powers in the Middle East, one Sunni and the other Shiite, are fundamentally competitors for power and influence. There is no better evidence to that effect than the two respective visits of the two leaders to Lebanon in 2010. President of Iran Mahmoud Ahmadinejad came to Lebanon and had a dialogue with the Shiite community. Erdoğan came to Lebanon and spoke to the Sunni community. Everyone in the Middle East who reads the recent polls on the relative popularity of different leaders in the Arab street noticed first the comparison between Erdoğan on one side, and Ahmadinejad and Lebanese Secretary General Hassan Nasrallah on the other, and the rising popularity of the first at the expense of the latter.[2]

The fact that Turkey is not using hard power in its competition for leadership and influence with Iran, but only soft power, is masking the fact that Turkey is engaged in hard competition with Iran. While Iran uses threats of violence, subversion, and incitement, Turkey uses economy and diplomacy; and it seems that the Turkish model is more attractive.

In this context, Turkey has no interest in Iran becoming a nuclear power. It may have opinions that are different from those of Israel or Western powers on the effective strategies that might prevent Iran's progress toward a status as a nuclear power, but that does not indicate that the purpose of its policies is to help Iran gain this status.

The leadership and the elites in Turkey perceive its special position—a country that is positioned between Europe and the Middle East, between West and East—as an important asset of its soft power. Turkey wishes to be on good terms with all the actors and to play the role of intermediary among them. In that way, it can play a more significant diplomatic role and, at the same time, deal with some root causes for instability in the Middle East that are perceived by the Turks as undermining their interests. Turkey tries to play the role of a power for stability in the Middle East, although not always successfully, while Iran plays the role of a power of instability in the Middle East. Turkey very much liked the position it occupied as an intermediary between Israel and Syria in 2008, when Prime Minister Ehud Olmert was interested in resuming negotiations with Syria with the mediation of Turkey. Israel's experience of the role it played was also positive. Turkey fulfilled very well the role of an honest broker.

Even in the present crisis and under the present circumstances, Turkey still manifests interest in keeping a relationship with Israel and playing a mediating role between it and its Arab neighbors. Turkey did not break its diplomatic relations with Israel after the *Mavi Marmara* incident, although its ambassador was called back to Ankara, and economic relations are to a large extent back to normal.[3] The domain most affected by the crisis in the

---

2. This competition is also having negative implications for Israel because of the convenience of using attacks on Israel as a way to gain popularity in the Arab street.

3. Based on data presented by Dan Katrivas of the Israeli Association of the Industrialists in a conference on "The Role of Economics in Peacemaking in the

relations has been that of security cooperation. Israeli military training in Turkey and Turkish military training in Israel stopped completely, no new weapons deals have been negotiated, and one can assume that the more secret and sensitive areas of cooperation were also badly hurt. There is also no improvement yet in the political relationship between the two states, though there is a continuous dialogue[4] between them aiming at finding a formula that will settle the issue of the *Mavi Marmara* incident. So far this dialogue is not bearing fruit, and the impression on the Israeli side in the lead-up to the Turkish elections of June 2011 was that there was no real possibility of an agreement between the two sides before the coming elections in Turkey because the crisis with Israel was a useful tool for Erdoğan during the election campaign.

In the meantime, the Arab Middle East, and possibly also Iran, are going through a stormy period of change that started with the popular revolution in Tunisia and led also to the downfall of President Hosni Mubarak and a change of regime in Egypt. The chairs of many Arab governments are shaking, and sensitivity to popular moods and public opinion all over the Middle East is growing. It is uncertain what effect these developments will have on the Israeli-Turkish relationship. Although there are enormous uncertainties as to the possible results of these earthquakes, some initial possible implications can be pointed at:

- U.S. status and power in the Middle East will be further eroded, which implies that the United States will have less influence on Turkish policies.
- The two new contenders for power in the Middle East, Turkey and Iran, have more opportunities to acquire influence because of the volatile situation in the Arab Middle East, and they will probably try to shape these developments in a way that will further advance their interests.
- There will probably be a sharp competition between the two models of change, the Turkish model and the Iranian model. So far it seems that the Turkish model has a clear advantage. The revolts in

Middle East" that took place at Oxford University on February 7, 2011. According to this data, the trade between the two states in 2010 returned to the level of 2008 before the reduction in 2009 following the crisis in the relations between the two states.

4. Part of which is a formal dialogue between the two governments, and the other is a use of Track II channels.

the Arab world were initiated and led by Westernized youth, and the Islamists were lagging behind. The demands are for freedom, democracy, transparency, and decent government. That does not mean necessarily that the balance between the two will not change through time because of the advantages of the radical Islamists in organization, ruthlessness, and better competence in harnessing faith for political purposes.

- On the other hand, if Egypt succeeds in regaining stability, it may reemerge as a contestant for leadership in the Arab world. That might reignite competition with both Iran and Turkey.
- There will be an opportunity to develop new policies vis-à-vis the Gaza Strip, in which Turkey perceives it has strong interest, and some Turkish-Egyptian cooperation in this area is possible.

The main implication for Israel is that Turkey will be even more involved in the Middle East and with the Arab states and societies. This would be unlikely to improve Israeli-Turkish relations. On the more operational and tactical level, Egyptian-Turkish cooperation on Gaza will act against Israeli interests as long as Israel does not change its attitude toward Gaza.

On the other hand, the competition between Turkey and Iran and the potential competition between Egypt and these two states creates some room for Israel to maneuver among these competing powers in cooperation with the United States. This possible opportunity is conditioned on Israel's ability to change the atmosphere in its relationship with the Arab world by new peace initiatives. It is difficult to envisage Israel being capable of maneuvering in this space in a situation of growing enmity between it and its Arab neighbors. The latter situation would provide a fertile ground for Iran to expand its influence and its brand of change, while, for its part, Turkey would have no choice but to stand for the Arabs and against Israel. Otherwise, it would have no chance competing with Iran in the Arab world.

4

# Strategic Perspectives: Comments and Discussion

## *Ellen Laipson:*

What do we mean by "strategic"? The structure of today's discussion has been to look first at strategic considerations and then the domestic drivers. Yet virtually all of our speakers have interwoven internal and external factors. Can we really segment out strategic considerations from the day-to day domestic politics of these three countries? Though it is used in different ways, to me sometimes "strategic" means a consideration that endures over time. It has a long-lasting structural importance to how a country sees itself in the world. But "strategic" can also mean a very intense interest in a given issue at a single point in time, and this can trump other issues in intensity and importance. These three countries show that domestic forces can acquire a strategic importance and become either a constraint on leaders or an accelerator of how we think about the national interest of a particular country. The domestic and international spheres of politics appear to be interwoven.

Whether the Turkish-Israeli relationship has been up or down has often depended on the views of the elites in those countries at a given time, and has been very much tied to perceptions of whether the United States is on the rise or in decline. Much of what we have heard shows that the rise and decline of powers and the redistribution of power since the end of the Cold War cannot be ignored. Each of these stories has a dimension to it that is about shifts in power.

I want to pick up on a couple of points that the earlier speakers made. Part of the story is about Turkey's strategic competition with Iran and how Israel and the United States adapt to it. Israel and the United States get rattled when Turkey appears friendly with Iran, but they fail to understand that Turkey has its own balancing act to play. Turkey is trying to maintain relations with Iran, which is in some ways a peer competitor, but at the same time a country that lags far behind Turkey according to many indicators of national power and development. Although Turkey's competition with Iran can benefit the United States and Israel in the long run, sometimes the latter two countries overreact to points of friction and perceived divergences with Turkey. An example of this occurred when Turkey worked with Brazil to try to get Iran to agree on a nuclear package. Even though Turkey was working on behalf of Western preferences, it was still seen in Washington as too soft on Iran.

Greg Gause's remarks reminded me that we keep coming back to Iraq as a player that illuminates some of these tensions and potentials for cooperation. In the mid-1990s, Turkey and the United States worked together

---

*The domestic and international spheres of politics appear to be interwoven.*

---

to try to settle an Iraqi Kurdish civil war. I participated in these U.S.-led talks, while working in the White House at the time. In the end, though, just when it appeared that a deal would be reached, Turkey backed out because it could not accede to any settlement that appeared to strengthen Kurdish unity. Their own perceptions of the Kurds vis-à-vis the future of Iraq were divergent from American interests.

Now, Israel was not a party to those talks, but it saw the Kurds as being among their non-Arab partners in the world (the legacy of former Prime Minister David Ben Gurion), along with Turkey, Iran, and Ethiopia. Thus, Israel was a silent player on behalf of keeping the Kurds capable, autonomous, and less threatened. This was in strong contrast to Turkey's position, which has evolved quite a bit since that moment of panic.

Regarding Soli Özel's remarks, I am on the side that believes that Turkey has gained strategic value and reestablished itself as a key player, more so compared to the Cold War. The United States likes the idea of Turkey as a bridge country, but it still does not quite know how to cope with an independent Turkey that may have interests different from our own. With the end of the Cold War, it does appear that Turkey is up and Israel is down, though the latter is not down in all respects.

Regarding Shlomo Brom's remarks, it is true that Turkey and Israel have different views of the Middle East region in terms of their own interests. Turkey does see the Middle East as an arena to show that it can be a regional power and a global actor. Turkey is a rising middle power in a cluster of countries that are increasingly important, like Indonesia and Brazil. Israel, however, is isolated right now. It may have a technocratic niche in the global system, but it does not have any natural alliances in the world, and it is not as important politically as it was in the past. In a period where relative power is being redistributed, Turkey's rise and Israel's defensiveness are evident. What still needs to be addressed is the decline of the United States' relative power and its ability to act as an agent of change in the region.

## *Philip Zelikow:*

Thinking of the U.S.-Israeli-Turkish strategic triangle, I want to point out that relations among nations are conjured and constructed. They are abstractions. They are metaphors. Beneath all the elaborate talk about foreign policy, what actually exist are narrow streams of interactions conducted among a handful of elite participants, which characterize many

---

*. . . relations among nations are conjured and constructed. They are abstractions. They are metaphors.*

---

diplomatic moves among nations. It is hard not to feel a sense of uneasiness when large labels are imposed on these narrow streams of interaction. It is problematic to apply grand theories to what is happening, because events defy generalization. I'd like to talk about what this means for U.S. relations with Turkey and Israel.

U.S. foreign relations, especially with Turkey, but also with Israel and almost all countries, are inductive and reactive. People should be wary of things like the Bush Doctrine and other grand strategies, which are thought up to lend coherence to things that are largely the products of idiosyncratic reactive choices, prompted by whatever happened to plunge into someone's in-box at the moment. It may be the case that Turkish foreign policy is guided by grand strategies and broad coherent objectives, but I do not think that is a satisfactory way to describe U.S. foreign policy. Now, let me turn to some key interactions between the United States and Turkey. They are not very well known, and they haven't really been discussed so far in much detail. Let me give you seven illustrations.

- The first illustration: The Gulf War of 1990-91. I was involved in U.S.-Turkish relations right from the start of this, working as a career Foreign Service Officer. I accompanied Secretary of State James Baker on his trip to Ankara in August 1990. We needed Turkey to be a front-line state in this confrontation, and we needed Turkey to take an economic hit, because one of the principal outlets for Iraq's oil products went through Turkey, and this was a great source of revenue for the Turkish state. The United States wanted Turkey to cut off that outlet immediately, with promises for later financial compensation. The United States also wanted Turkey to go along with a NATO action that it was seeking approval of in Brussels. The implication was that Turkey would have to host allied aircraft against Iraq on behalf of NATO, thus becoming a cobelligerent in the war. Others have noted high levels of U.S.-Turkish cooperation during this period.
- The second illustration: Cooperation with NATO in all of the crises involving Muslims in the Balkans during the 1990s. This is a tangled story, but suffice it to say that Turkey's role was constructive.
- The third illustration: The issues in the Transcaucasus region after the breakup of the Soviet Union. These are issues in which Turkey is very concerned and involved. Again, Turkey's role has been constructive, despite historical problems with Azerbaijanis and Armenians.
- The fourth illustration: Turkey's aspirations for EU membership, which the United States has supported as a deliberate decision over a number of years. Part of the U.S. position has to do with respecting Turkish choices about how they wish to define their identity, and Turkey has done an enormous amount to make itself eligible for EU membership. Whether or not Turkey's accession to the European Union ever comes to fruition, what the Turks did with U.S. support to become eligible for membership is an encouraging story.
- The fifth illustration: The soft power of Turkey post-9/11 in the Muslim world. Rather than the clash of civilizations between the

West and Islam, the clash within Islamic civilization about what it will become is one of the defining struggles of this age. Turkey is obviously an important protagonist in that story. Turkish business, TV melodramas, and construction magnates are all over the Arab and Muslim world, and Americans regard this Turkish presence as basically positive, though there is some dispute about this among American elites.

- The sixth illustration: The Iraq War since 2003 and Turkey's very important role in that. Turkey's initial refusal to cooperate by not allowing the U.S. Fourth Infantry Division to pass through its territory into Iraq is well-known, but actually not that important. The big deal involves Kurdistan, and Turkey has had to make some tough choices there. This is a very difficult and important story, as anybody familiar with the role of the Kurds in the development of the modern Turkish nation-state will know. Meanwhile, the Kurdish issue inside Iraq is very important too. Americans are trying to walk a tightrope, one in which the Kurds, who would prefer to declare an independent state and secede from Iraq, do not do that, but at the same time gain an adequate degree of autonomy. Meanwhile, the Kurds have an uneasy relation to the PKK-led Kurdish insurrection inside Turkey itself. Many details of U.S.-Turkish cooperation regarding the Kurdish issue are still secret, but there has been much constructive work done on some very sensitive matters over the past seven years.
- The seventh illustration: Finally, of course, there's the issue of Iran, and Turkey's attitudes toward Ahmadinejad, which are too friendly from the point of view of the United States, though not quite dangerous. There has, nevertheless, been some constructive cooperation.

Now, let's turn to U.S.-Israeli relations. I will spend very little time on this because this is a story that I think is well understood, having been much more in the public eye. The correlation with the Cold War is rough at best, enjoying a convergence from the mid-1960s to the mid-1980s, especially in the early 1980s. The relationship has been increasingly problematic from 2005 and 2006. If you examine the specific content of that relationship, what are the issues that appear in the in-boxes of American policymakers that have to do with Israel? There are some things that involve constructive cooperation—technological innovation, or global financial cooperation. There has been important constructive cooperation on some issues to do with Iran (though Israel would be taking the initiative on this issue by itself, if necessary). But mainly, U.S. policymakers encounter issues involving Israel in the defensive part of their in-box, under damage control and danger control. The Israelis are not able to play a very active role on many issues that go beyond Israel.

Now, let's step back from all that has been discussed and think about the broader content of these relationships. I don't see much of a strategic triangle, except as an evanescent metaphor of the 1990s. If it is an inductive, reactive story, issues come in as defensive issues or constructive issues. U.S.-Israeli relations are very broad in the public consciousness, but their content is increasingly quite narrow and defensive. The U.S.-Turkish relationship is almost nonexistent in public consciousness, but increasingly strong among elites, and the scope of its constructive relationships is broad and broadening. Think about the scope of issues in which Turkey is constructively involved with the United States—geographically, regionally, in subject matter, hard power, and soft power—and you begin to see the range of the issues that come into the in-box concerning Turkey and the contrast between that and U.S.-Israeli relations.

*U.S. policymakers encounter issues involving Israel in the defensive part of their in-box, under damage control and danger control.*

## *Brantly Womack:*

My task here today is to relate this very complex set of relationships among three countries to more general thinking about international relationships. This is very difficult, because we have three interrelated and significant relationships, but none of them is the most important for any single party. The closest might be Turkey-United States or United States-Israel, but that is not true for both sides of the relationship. We have a situation where other relationships are going to be affecting these particular relationships. They are in a region, which not only defies definition, but is also a vortex of vital global concerns, such as energy, and considerable unrest. It is as if we are looking at three noodles in a bowl of spaghetti, and we're thinking, "Well, if we shake the bowl, where are they going to go?" It's not even clear where they were, much less where they are going to go. So, how do we bring theoretical clarity, what kinds of theoretical issues can we raise here?

The key factor is uncertainty and the problem of dealing with it. For all three nations, their next action will not determine a definite future or prevent a definite future. From my more distant perspective, the three nations have fundamentally different approaches to coping with uncertainty. The United States, as the global actor involved, attempts to economize its attention, rather than "staring" at the situation for too long. So it manages its attention by stereotyping nations into friends and enemies, which is most obvious in the United States' Iran policy (and hard to change). Doing this simplifies the world for leaders who have more important things to deal with. It deals with red lines and crises.

Ellen Laipson made a good point about "strategic" having two meanings, and one of the meanings being a key meaning. From the point of view of a global actor, that difference is very important. A global actor has strategic views that are self-generated, and then when crises arise, those become strategic because they rise to the point of necessary action by the global actor. Thus, from the U.S. point of view, we often don't know

*For the United States, the world is becoming multinodal.*

there are trees until they fall. Our attention is on the crisis and resolving it, rather than understanding what led to the crisis. The roots of crises are beneath America's attention as a global actor. I think this factor is reflected in all three papers presented today by Gause, Özel, and Brom, especially regarding the end of the Cold War. Did the Cold War's end transform policy? Perhaps not, but it did change the context in which the crises that occurred in the area, and the practical diplomacy used to handle them, changed.

So, what is Turkey's policy? The "zero problems" policy addresses the problem of uncertainty in a very distinctive way. It tries to minimize conflict, establishing a framework for deflecting and defusing crises. In a sense, this is not all that different from Turkey's old policy of working with Israel and Iran against the Arab world. In effect, Turkey has brought that caution home in dealing with other immediate neighbors. I see a change in where that policy gets applied. I don't see the "zero problems" policy as an attempt to build an alliance of its neighbors against distant enemies. Thus, it only threatens the relationship with Israel by displacement, rather than by creating a new hostile alliance.

Israel's approach is to minimize its exposure to risk, and this means expanding the circle of suspects. This leads Israel, perhaps, into a situation of greater isolation. But it builds its defense against uncertainty by being able to defend itself, to build barricades, to develop weaponry, and to forge relationships with the major powers that will enable it to prevail in any possible conflict.

What are the problems with each of these? For the United States, the world is becoming multinodal. I don't say multipolar, because the world is becoming far more complex than that. There is no set of countries that can do what a superpower once thought it could do. Power and capacities matter, but they do not determine a situation of control. We are dealing with a situation of proliferating complexities with limited capacities. The result is that we don't get closure on international problems, and yet we continue to see them as important. I don't see this as a problem of Obama's indecisiveness; rather, it's a question of the lagged consequences of George W. Bush's overreach. Now, some yearn for the Cold War and look to China as the new Soviet Union, but China is merely the lead point in this multinodal world, and it will not be the new Soviet Union. The United States will not have a containment option with China. So, China is a general sign of other nations being more autonomous in their decision-making, and the United States having less power to control that.

What are the problems that Turkey faces? Like China, the problem for Turkey is how to develop normalcy in international relationships, despite continuing differences of interest. It is not "zero problems," it is continual negotiations over interests in a transformative situation. Success has built confidence in Turkey, but it does not preempt contested interests. For Turkey, the essence of policy is trying to minimize conflict.

Israel faces the problem of self-isolation because of its risk-avoiding approach to uncertainty, making it more and more dependent on relations with the United States. As Professor Brom pointed out, Israel does not want to become a regional power. Yes, but part of that is because Israel does not want to become a true member of the region. Israel is not ambitious, but it is kind of ornery when it comes to the rest of the region. If this is the situation, then the isolation of Israel is a definite problem. In my neck of the woods, some people have called Taiwan "Asia's Israel." I think Israel must be careful not to become the "Middle East's Taiwan." Taiwan has become a burden on U.S. diplomacy, and people are becoming uncomfortable with it. Thus, the implications of what Philip Zelikow was saying about the defensive nature of the U.S.-Israeli relationship also pose a danger to Israel.

## Discussion:

**Soli Özel:** When Turks look at the world, they see themselves as more and more important as a regional player, sometimes conflictual with the United States, but nonetheless there is a conflation of interests so long as the United States respects our autonomy. To a certain extent this comes, as far as the Turks are concerned, at the expense of Israel. Given Israel's power in the domestic politics of the United States, how the United States adjusts itself to this new framework, its ability to prevail upon Israel to change the way it relates to the region, and whether Israel wishes to be truly situated in the region—all these points (especially the last) strike me as big issues.

Secondly, I've been thinking about the turbulence in our region, particularly in Syria, which is the "Humpty Dumpty" of the region. I wonder how Israel can afford not to establish normalized relations with Turkey. If Syria explodes, it will have an impact on all surrounding countries. This would be the kind of emergency that would necessitate a dialogue among all parties that surround Syria, especially Israel and Turkey. The fact that segments in Israel will block this dialogue because Israel will not apologize (or come close to pretending to apologize) for *Mavi Marmara*, strikes me as very shortsighted, and ultimately dangerous, not just for Israel, but for all the regional powers and for the greater stability of the region.

**William Quandt:** I've been reading the Israeli and Turkish press. Both seem worried by the prospect that Syrian President Bashar al-Asad might go. In other words, stability under a dictator like Asad has some virtues. He is a known quantity for Israel—not friendly, but it is the quietest border they face. And with Turkey, it is quite a friendly relationship with the Asad regime, or at least it has been.

**Soli Özel:** What is truly intriguing here is that the movement from which our current ruling party (in Turkey) comes has, during the entirety of its career, hated the Syrian regime because the latter would not tolerate the Muslim Brotherhood and, of course, the legacy of the Hama massacre of 1982. And ideologically, the ruling party in Turkey should favor the rise of the opposition in Syria, but realistically they have invested so much in the current regime they cannot readily let it go.

**Shlomo Brom:** Regarding the last point, the devil that you know is better than the devil that you do not know. Along with my American colleagues, I would say that strategies are an attempt to rationalize policies that usually come at a later stage. I would also say that Israeli policies are also mostly reactive/defensive, whatever you might call it. I was there when Israel's relations with Turkey got better at the beginning of the 1990s, and this didn't start with a strategy. It started with de facto decisions in relation to an agenda at a certain moment, and then it developed into a kind of strategy. So Philip Zelikow makes a valid point.

---

*. . . strategies are an attempt to rationalize policies that usually come at a later stage.*

---

I am a person who believes the present Israeli policies are wrong, and that Israel should open up to the region, certainly in the current situation. Given our isolation before, and the turmoil in the region now, with all of its uncertainty, Israel risks losing its few remaining "relative" friends. You know, everything is relative, so now we are talking about Egypt's Mubarak as a friend. I remember a few years ago, we were complaining about the difficult peace we were having with Egypt. So, we have to open up, but for that we need some domestic political changes that I hope will take place.

**William Quandt:** We haven't heard much discussion about what used to be called the Arab-Israeli peace process, and yet Turkey was being quite helpful during 2008 in the Syrian-Israeli track before things went sour. Does either Shlomo Brom or Soli Özel envisage a possibility that if Bashar al-Asad manages to ride out the storm, or if there is a change that brings a more pragmatic regime to Syria, that Turkey might resume its role as a broker, or would it no longer be interested or necessary?

**Soli Özel:** Well first of all, the fact that Turkey had relations with Israel was very good for everybody else concerned because it could adjudicate things, relay messages, and so forth, since it was proven that the relationship was not used against third parties. Therefore, when the Turkish government reacted the way it did to Gaza in late 2008 and early 2009, and basically all communications broke down (the Syrians also withdrew themselves), Turkey lost an important asset in terms of its diplomacy and its presence. The Turkish prime minister took this personally because he believed he had come very close to brokering an agreement between Syria and Israel, but then the Gaza incident occurred, and he was caught unaware, and he looked almost complicit in the Israeli offensive.

Now the Turkish side argues that at the beginning of May 2010, U.S. peace negotiator George Mitchell asked the Turkish side to see if they could reactivate the Syrian track of the peace process. This is what the planned meeting in Washington (prior to the *Mavi Marmara* incident) between U.S. Secretary of State Hillary Clinton and Turkish Foreign Minister Ahmet Davutoğlu was supposed to have been about. In that context, there are plenty of Turks who believe that a deal had been struck with the Israelis as to how to manage the stopping of the *Mavi Marmara*, but the Israeli story is very different. Nonetheless, had the incident not taken place, Clinton and Davutoğlu would have met, and there are a lot of people in Turkey who believe that segments in the Israeli polity actually wanted to block improvements in relations. Whether that is true or just conspiratorial thinking, there are circumstantial reasons to think it is not implausible. Therefore, I think Turkey would be very interested in again becoming a broker, but there is this apology issue.

**Shlomo Brom:** Well, if you ask most Israelis now they would say "never again" because the emotional response to what happened in the Israeli-Turkish relationship is very high. The perceptions are totally different on the two sides. The perception on the Turkish side regarding the *Mavi Marmara* incident is that the Turkish government is an innocent bystander, that it was a ship with well-wishing, peace-loving people aboard, and all they wanted was to bring food to starving people in Gaza. The perception in Israel is that it was assisted and initiated by the Turkish government, and that they allowed a group of fanatical, violent, armed Islamists to board the ship. That is the reason for the results. It is due to completely different perceptions. In my opinion, the problem is not aversion to apologizing about the flotilla incident on Israel's part. The problem is completely divorced perceptions of what went wrong and who is respon sible for what.

By the way, Israel does not refuse to apologize to Turkey about the incident, so long as Turkey also apologizes and takes its share of responsibility for what happened. And there it is stuck. But nevertheless, I say, "never say never," though actually at the present moment, the Israeli government doesn't want negotiations with Syria. It is not a question on the agenda at all. But I can certainly see a change of circumstances that might lead an Israeli government to reopen negotiations with Syria—usually this happens when negotiations with the Palestinians are completely stuck and there is an urge to do something, then we go to Syria. And then, once again, the possibility of using the good services of the Turkish government will be raised, because factually they did a very good job when this mediation was taking place.

**Soli Özel:** One point of information. When the Mount Carmel forest fires occurred in Israel, Turkey made a goodwill gesture by sending two firefighting airplanes, and Prime Minister Netanyahu unexpectedly went to greet the crews. And thereupon, the two sides had their officials meet in Geneva, and presumably there was an understanding. But that never really went anywhere. I suppose, on the Turkish side, there is a willingness to get this current problem solved because of the costs attached to it in the United States, whereas whether the kind of willingness on the Israeli side is as strong—this I doubt.

**Questioner:** Professor Gause, I believe your last comment was that Israel is an obvious strategic ally of the United States. It seems apparent to me that Israel is as important in the American domestic sphere as it is to our foreign relations. But it seems that there are not many issues now in which Israel is of primary interest. Could you please clarify the most important issues of concern in the Middle East region right now, and if possible how they might be resolved following the Arab uprisings?

**F. Gregory Gause, III:** I think the U.S.-Israeli relationship is based on a profound, and extremely variegated, interaction of elites in societies. I do not think it is driven by strategic concerns at all. In the post–Cold War world, we have seen that various American administrations have decided that the peace process is not all that central anymore—largely because of the removal of the Arab oil weapon from the calculations of Arab-Israeli conflict. We have had three post-Cold War administrations, and one (Clinton) put an enormous effort into the peace process, but apparently didn't think it was important enough to bang heads because they were willing to walk away from the process in 2000 with absolutely no gains. Then we had an administration (George W. Bush) that didn't think the peace process was important for anything except cosmetics, and we have an administration

*. . . the U.S.-Israeli relationship has almost nothing to do with what is actually going on in the Middle East. It has a lot more to do with these extremely close ties between our two societies.*

now (Obama) that seemed to think that movement on Israeli-Palestinian issues was vitally important, deliberately engaged in a confrontation with Israel over settlements as one of its first foreign policy actions, but backed away when it saw no benefits and saw it was paying some costs.

So it seems to me that the U.S.-Israeli relationship has almost nothing to do with what is actually going on in the Middle East. It has a lot more to do with these extremely close ties between our two societies. That is the way it is, but that does not mean the Israelis do not want the United States to help out in certain ways and take certain positions. Israel will want the United States to do certain things, and the latter will have to isolate its relationship with Israel from all of the other things it has to do in the region. I think that is the pattern we have seen since the Gulf War of 1990-91, and I think that will continue when all of what is happening in the Arab world settles down.

**Questioner:** I have a question primarily for Professor Özel. We've been talking about inductive and reactive foreign policy coming out of the United States. I have looked at Foreign Minister Davutoğlu and Prime Minister Erdoğan's foreign policy, and at least in theory it was very deductive and proactive. You have mentioned Turkey's relationship with Syria, but talk for a bit about Egypt and Libya, where it was only six or seven weeks ago that President Abdullah Gül of Turkey had a visit to Egypt, and now we have had a whole change of actors in Egypt. It seems to be a situation where Turkey will have to be a bit more inductive and reactive in trying to reconstitute relations with countries that have had dramatic changes, Egypt and Libya in particular.

**Soli Özel:** I was taught two things: One, to think structurally about international relations, independent of inclinations and theories. Second, that foreign policy, as opposed to international relations, was 80 percent about reacting to things. Foreign policy is not just a function of induction and reaction, but it's a big part. Professor Davutoğlu, who is a rather rigid structuralist, is learning the hard way that you can try to will the world in your mind, and the world will just not bend to your will.

On January 3rd of this year, Davutoğlu spoke to the assembled ambassadors of Turkey. He said it was not enough for Turkey to be a firefighter. It had to be more of an urban planner to prevent fires, a kind of wise country and order setter. That is very audacious and very ambitious, and life has a way of telling you that you are going way above what is rational and possible.

Now, President Gül went to Egypt after Mubarak was gone. Just as Davutoğlu went to Tunisia, this was a way to say that Turkey supported the new regime and would be ready to provide help. The Turkish prime minister was the first person to call on Mubarak to leave. Turkey acted before anyone else on this. It did not do much regarding Tunisia, but on Libya, Turkey has gone from asking what business NATO had in Libya to bragging about the fact that it now has four frigates, one submarine, and so forth contributing to the effort, and that a command and control center is in Izmir. So, Turkey is reacting to things. And on Syria, Turkey is totally caught between its investment in the regime and its inclination to support the opposition. This is how it is going to be. You will see more realism in Turkish foreign policy, even rhetorically. Given President Asad's very tough stance, Turkey will have to forget about influencing the outcome and just watch what is happening in Syria on an issue that is very important for them.

PART II

# Perspective of the Obama Administration

*In planning this gathering, I thought it important to have the Obama administration's point of view on relations with Turkey and Israel presented directly. We were fortunate to have Principal Deputy Assistant Secretary of State for European and Eurasian Affairs Tina S. Kaidanow make this contribution. Ambassador Kaidanow was an excellent choice, since she had long experience in dealing with issues in the Balkans, served as ambassador to Kosovo, and was Director of Southeast Asian Affairs at the National Security Council. In these capacities, she has had extensive dealings with Turkey, and it was the topic of U.S.-Turkish relations that was the focus of her remarks.*

*(We had earlier been hoping that Undersecretary of State for Political Affairs William Burns, a senior career diplomat with long experience in the Middle East, could be with us. But just before the conference convened, we learned that Burns was being promoted to the position of Deputy Secretary of State and would be unable to come to Charlottesville.)*

*We reproduce here the text of Ambassador Kaidanow's official remarks as she delivered them. The reader will see an intelligence and a frankness that those at the gathering much appreciated and that was also evident during the off-the-record session she later participated in, along with the other conference participants.*

~ *WBQ*

5

# The U.S.-Turkish Relationship: A View from the Obama Administration

*Tina S. Kaidanow,*
*Bureau of Euopean and Eurasian Affairs*

Good morning everyone, first of all, I apologize on behalf of Under Secretary Burns, that he can't be here this morning. He very much did want to come and address you all, but as Dr. Quandt said, he is a little bit busy this week. And he has been a little bit busy for a number of weeks. Because there is a lot going on, not just obviously in North Africa and the Middle East, but across the globe, and his job very much involves all of those issues. My focus is a little bit more narrow, so I will make a few prepared remarks if you will allow me, primarily as Dr. Quandt noted on the U.S.-Turkish relationship, but a little bit more broad than that, and then afterwards I understand there will be a question and answer and you can vigorously disagree with what I say or agree with it as you like. First of all again, thank you for having me here today.

Today's topic, the U.S.-Turkey-Israel strategic relationship or "strategic triangle," is extremely timely, I think, in light of all the events in the region. If you'll allow me, I'll talk about our relationship with Turkey, I'll touch on our relationship with Israel, which again I have to say right up front is not my primary area of expertise, and then I'll comment a little bit on why the administration views relations between the two, between Israel and Turkey, as important for the region as a whole. Finally, I'll share some thoughts with you on the regional shifts that are now taking place, what they might mean for all of us, and how we see Turkey engaging as a new dynamic takes hold in the region.

First, let me talk just briefly about the U.S.-Turkey relationship.

I have to say right up front that there are few governments with whom we have a more ongoing and open dialogue than the government of Turkey. We believe that an active, engaged, and collaborative relationship with Turkey is really an important interest of the United States, and of Turkey. Our common interests range from political to military to economic and far beyond. The benefits of the U.S.-Turkey relationship are very much mutual in our view, and are based on a long-term partnership that is strong, although it has weathered some various short-term bumps in the road.

Turkey is an integral part of the Euro-Atlantic alliance, and it has been for decades. Turkey became a member of NATO in 1952 and has distinguished itself as a military ally ever since that time. Turkey has the second largest standing army within NATO, which I think people sometimes forget. Turkey has stood shoulder to shoulder with the United States from Korea to Kosovo to Kabul. In the most recent example of Libya, Turkey helped evacuate American personnel at the outset of that crisis and has agreed to be our protecting power in Tripoli. And now, Turkey is poised to take on additional responsibilities as a NATO ally in pursuit of the various mandates provided for under UN Resolutions 1970 and 1973.

In recent years, Turkey has pursued an increasingly active foreign policy and is engaging much more intensively than ever before with countries across its neighborhood and beyond. Much of this activism is no doubt fueled by one of the highest economic growth rates in the region, or in the world—8.5 percent last year, which I think is very truly impressive when

---

*. . . there are few governments with whom we have a more ongoing and open dialogue than the government of Turkey.*

---

you consider that many of the world's economies were contracting during that same period. Turkey is a member of the G20, and aspires to be a "top ten" economy by 2020. To meet those goals, Turkey has aggressively pursued new export markets, and the economic dynamism that Turkey has pursued is at least in part a driver of Turkey's increased diplomatic engagement on the world stage. So, I think in some ways we can see this new diplomatic energy from Turkey as an effort to bring its global leadership profile more in line with its emerging economic status.

In its desire to find new export markets and increase its leadership profile, Turkey is reaching out to the countries in its region, including its neighbors to the east, occasionally in ways that some in the West question Turkey's traditional, let's call it, Western orientation. There has been much discussion in various circles of whether Turkey is "drifting" or "turning" from the West towards a new, and somehow more problematic, "Eastern" vocation.

We believe, the United States government believes, and I think the Turks would agree as well, that the notion that Turkey must somehow choose between East and West is really a question that is falsely posed. We are convinced that Turkey's EU accession process is a net positive for both Turkey and for Europe, encouraging Turkish reform and promising to enhance mutually beneficial relations between Turkey and Europe. At the same time, however, Turkey has legitimate interests in pursuing better relations with its eastern neighbors, whether in the immediate neighborhood or even beyond that. The United States has been, and continues to be, supportive of this; in fact, while some have criticized Turkey for emphasizing their eastward relations, we understand that Turkey's ties in places like Afghanistan, Pakistan, Iraq, and Libya are all helpful in advancing our shared goals.

In Iraq, for example, close coordination with Turkey has been an essential element in assisting the formation of a stable and representative government in Baghdad. Turkey has improved its relations with the Kurdistan Regional Government in Iraq's north, which is an important component of stability there, and Turkish engagement in Iraq's economic sector is also helping to advance our common objective of economic development and growth. In Afghanistan, Turkey's contributions are equally significant: Turkey is the largest troop contributor to ISAF among the OIC countries; it commands two PRTs, which some of you know are provincial reconstruction teams; and it has trained thousands of Afghan security forces. Turkey has also made significant contributions to stabilization efforts in Pakistan.

But let me be equally frank, and say that despite the many, many areas of convergence, maintaining strong relations between the United States and Turkey can sometimes be a challenge. Turkey can and does take different views on some issues than we do. Our two countries have from time to time employed different tactics, and we have had disagreements.

On Iran, for example, we were disappointed that Turkey voted against the June 2010 UN resolution imposing sanctions on Iran. We've been very clear that unless Iran meets its international obligations on the nuclear issue and agrees to engage productively with the IAEA and the international community, sanctions must remain an important and integral element of the international response. Since Turkey's "no" vote on United Nations Security Resolution 1929, Turkey's leaders have nevertheless declared their commitment to abide by the resolution's terms, and they have continued to support efforts to reach a diplomatic resolution to international concerns about Iran's nuclear program.

Our ability to discuss this kind of difference directly with Turkey and build on our common goals is a hallmark, we think, of a mature bilateral relationship. Given the increasingly complex challenges that the world obviously faces, it is clear, to us anyway, that U.S.-Turkish cooperation is going to be more important than ever before.

I should also mention that in June, Turkey will hold parliamentary elections. Obviously, decisions about Turkey's political future can and must only be made by Turks within the context of Turkey's democratic system. But as a friend, we care about the ongoing development of successful, open democracy in Turkey. The process of reform and modernization that is so vital to Turkey's future does remain an important priority, for us and I think for Turkey. I'll return to that theme because I think it is important in the context of the larger context of regional developments as well.

As I noted at the top of my presentation, I am not an expert on the U.S.-Israel relationship, but I think there is no question that we believe those relations are really central to our strategic relations. As you well know, the United States was the first country to recognize Israel in 1948, and a strong commitment to Israel's security and well-being has been a cornerstone of U.S. policy in the Middle East ever since. We remain fully committed to Israel's security, and we remain committed to stability in the region, which includes a comprehensive, lasting Middle East peace.

Turkey has supported Middle East peace efforts in the past and served at one point as an important interlocutor between Israel and Syria.

But unfortunately, as we know, Turkish-Israeli relations have badly deteriorated. We have been dismayed and disheartened to see the breakdown of the once-critical strategic relationship between Turkey and Israel, which dates back to 1949, when Turkey was also one of the first countries to recognize the State of Israel. The two countries worked together to strengthen their economic, political, and military ties, leading to expanded investment and trade, close cooperation on security issues, and extensive people-to-people connections bolstered by travel and tourism. A constructive relationship between Turkey and Israel supports our interest in peace and stability in the region, and we cannot, therefore, obviously be indifferent to the course of relations between the two countries.

While we believe the tensions between Turkey and Israel are best resolved directly between them, we have encouraged and will continue to encourage both Turkey and Israel to undertake dialogue and move beyond the recent strains in their bilateral relationship. Both sides have told us that they want to move to their previously strong back-and-forth relationship. I think, however, it's important to be realistic and acknowledge that this will likely not be an overnight process. It will be up to Turkey and Israel to seek opportunities to engage bilaterally where their interests intersect and focus on the long-term benefits that improved relations can bring both countries.

Our relationship with each of these partners is based on much more than a calculation of interests—it is rooted in shared values and a shared vision. The United States and Turkey, and the United States and Israel, have made choices to establish these partnerships. With these partnerships come important responsibilities on all sides. Our three countries have broad and diverse interests, and we will not always see eye-to-eye on every issue. But we must never forget the larger outlook that we share. We share a vision of a democratic and secure Middle East, with a vibrant economy, integrated into the global community of nations.

And just to turn to the broader region for a moment, I don't have to tell obviously everyone here that the past few months we have seen really monumental shifts in the Middle East. It's exciting in many ways to watch the democratic impulses that are taking root across the region, but I think what is most striking to us is that the historic changes currently underway have really reaffirmed the consistent message we've given to all our partners: that security and stability are best achieved by governments that recognize the legitimate aspirations of their people. Our ability to realize our core interests in the region—achieving a just, comprehensive peace; lasting security between Israel and its neighbors; halting Iran's illicit nuclear activities and countering its use of violence and terrorism in support of its regional goals; supporting a sovereign, stable, self-reliant Iraq; countering terrorist groups; expanding trade and communications lines—all of that, in the long run, is enhanced by our ability to partner with ever more representative governments.

In the immediate term, for the aspirations of the people of Tunisia, Egypt, Libya, and beyond to be realized, the international community, and even more important, the close neighbors of these countries, have to play a supporting role. There has been quite a lot of discussion about whether, for example, Turkey can be a model with respect to democratic change and representative government. While certain elements of Turkey's democracy may be illustrative for countries in the region that are renewing or reinvigorating their democratic processes, we should be very clear, I think, that each country undergoing transition in the region has to choose the form of democracy that is best suited to its own people's legitimate demands. We hope that not only Turkey, but other democratic countries in the greater region and around the world, actually, will step forward to share best practices, encourage fledgling civil societies, and support their indigenous, homegrown efforts.

Of course, Libya is at the forefront of everyone's mind these days. As President Obama said on Monday night, "Forty years of tyranny has left Libya fractured and without strong civil institutions. The transition to a legitimate government that is responsive to the Libyan people will be, in fact, a very difficult task. And while the United States will do our part to help, it will be a task for the international community and—more—a task for the Libyan people themselves." This transition must come through an inclusive process, one that realizes and reflects the will of the Libyan people.

The United States is consulting closely with Turkey and other allies on the developments in Libya. Turkey has offered to play a key role in humanitarian assistance to Libya and is supporting NATO operations to enforce the UN Security Council resolution calling for a no-fly zone and the protection of civilians and civilian-populated areas. Just to come back for a moment to the central theme of this conference, the relationship between Turkey and Israel, I would stress again that among the uncertainties generated by the changes taking place in the region, seeing the Turkish-Israeli relationship back on a solid footing of friendship and partnership remains an enduring goal, one that has benefit for both of these countries as well as for us. We will continue to invest our efforts towards that objective, and we continue to urge both sides to come together as soon as they possibly can.

PART III

# Domestic Political Influences

*It is now widely understood that in democratic polities there is bound to be a significant influence of domestic politics in the formulation of foreign policy. Even realist scholars, who often decry such influences, are quick to acknowledge the politics that goes into all policymaking.*

*As with the topic of strategic perspectives, I sought the views of three scholars who had studied the link between domestic politics and foreign policy in their respective countries—and had also, to varying degrees, participated in the policy process. As it turned out, each of these authors has a particularly interesting personal history that gives him or her a distinctive perspective. Henri Barkey, who authored the chapter on the United States, is of Turkish origin, but has spent his academic and professional career in America. Because of his deep knowledge of the country of his birth, he is a frequent participant in debates in Washington over how to handle the U.S.-Turkish relationship. He has also served on the State Department's Policy Planning Staff. Readers will note that he moves back and forth in his essay from how policy is made in Washington to how it is made in Ankara. He has a sharp eye for errors made by each side of the U.S.-Turkish relationship.*

*Yaprak Gürsoy is a careful student of Turkish politics. Her doctoral dissertation, written at the University of Virginia, was a comparison of the role of the militaries in Greece and Turkey. (She is one of the rare Turkish scholars who has learned Greek and done research there.) At our gathering, she focused her attention on showing how Turkey's domestic politics has affected its relations with both Israel and the United States. Contrary to the views of many who write on this topic, she does not conclude that the AKP and its Islamist orientation have much to do with the changes of recent years. Instead, she sees Turkish policy as reflecting the country's growing economic power, the reduced role of its military, and the government's responses to regional changes. She notes that Turkish public opinion is highly nationalistic and that Prime Minister Erdoğan has been quite successful in winning support for his ambitious foreign policy, as shown by his success at the ballot box in recent elections.*

*Finally, Daniel Levy brought to the discussion of Israel's policy the experience of an insider who was on the Israeli negotiating team in talks with the Palestinians in 2000 as well as an Anglo-American-Israeli background that positions him well to address Israeli as well as American politics. Levy did not hesitate to point to the strong influence of the Israeli right wing generally in weakening the Israeli-Turkish link, and in particular to the role played by Foreign Minister Avigdor Lieberman. And he noted that Israel has been using its ties in Washington to pressure Turkey during this period of estrangement.*

*Two senior members of the University of Virginia Department of Politics, Professors Alan Lynch and Jeffrey Legro, were the lead commentators in this part of the discussion. Lynch is best known as a specialist on Russia and the former Soviet Union. But he is also a broad-gauged political analyst who teaches about the ties between domestic politics and foreign policy. In his contribution he examined the so-called "democratic peace" theory that leads us to expect that democracies such as the United States, Turkey, and Israel will enjoy good relations because of shared values. He urged us to consider, however, that the precondition for consolidating democratic norms is first to ensure regional peace. In a turbulent Middle East, it will take more than shared democratic values for nations to pursue congruent policies. If you want democracy to flourish, he argued, work for peace.*

*Finally, Legro is a well-known theorist who works on the role of ideas in international relations from a constructivist perspective. He urged us to think systematically about how to account for the weakening of the ties between the parties to this troubled triangular relationship. Without offering a clear explanation of his own, he noted that the various participants in the discussion had offered a wide range of different explanations, but not a single dominant one. He thereby helped set the stage for the lively discussion that followed—which I urge you to read and think about, for yourselves.*

*~WBQ*

6

# The Broken Triangle: How the U.S.-Israeli-Turkish Relationship Got Unglued

*Henri J. Barkey, Lehigh University*

The triangular relationship between the United States, Turkey, and Israel did not emerge until the end of the 1990s. The United States had previously viewed its relationship with these two countries quite separately. Starting with the deepening rapprochement of the late 1990s that saw an unprecedented cooperation between Jerusalem and Ankara, Washington, with both its executive and legislative branches, responded quickly. It not only welcomed these developments, but also made use of all opportunities to encourage the budding relationship. These efforts entailed economic cooperation, creation of Qualified Industrial Zones (QIZs), military exercises, some of which were extended to include Jordan, and search and rescue exercises. More importantly, perhaps, Washington came to view Turkey and Israel as enduring allies in a region where would-be hegemons, such as Iran and its allies, could be contained with their help.

Heralded as a strategic alliance that undid the traditional balance of power in the Middle East, the Israeli-Turkish relationship was never conceived as a bilateral one. From the beginning, it was Washington that would provide the incentive and glue for this emerging alliance. Without Washington in the distant picture, the Turkish authorities who were the prime movers would not have conceptualized it. At its pinnacle, the putative alliance was credited for forcing the Hafez al-Asad regime in Syria to kick Abdullah Öcalan, the Turkish Kurdish insurgent leader and head of the PKK, the Kurdistan Workers' Party, from his refuge in Damascus.

Hence the fracturing of the relationship starting in 2009 has come as a deep disappointment to Washington. It has put the Obama administration in a difficult if not impossible situation as both Israel and Turkey have looked for support for their positions. The rift between these two countries, however, is far deeper than anyone in Washington imagines and has already had serious repercussions affecting perceptions and policies. In many ways, Washington (as perhaps did Jerusalem) misread the nature of the Israeli-Turkish alliance and failed to comprehend the weak basis, especially in Turkey, underlying it.

## Origins

Ever since its founding, Israel has coveted relations with Turkey as part of what David Ben Gurion called the "periphery strategy": Israel's search for alliances with non-Arab states or groups, such as Iran, Turkey, Ethiopia, the Christians in Lebanon, and Iraqi Kurds, on the periphery of the Arab-Israeli conflict. This strategy helped break Israel's isolation and unnerved its opponents. In recent years, Turkey has also emerged as an important economic partner for Israel and, starting in the late 1990s, a crucial market for Israeli arms exports, an industry of vital national strategic importance. Moreover, Israeli leaders, especially Shimon Peres, the current president, also lobbied on behalf of Turkey's European Union accession project to ensure Ankara was solidly anchored in the West.

The recent origins of the relationship, however, go back to when Turgut Özal was prime minister and president (1983-1993). Özal, despite his conservative and pious background and leanings, was a quintessentially pro-American leader who prioritized his relationship with Washington over all others. He became prime minster following the return to civilian rule after the 1980-83 military interregnum. Anxious to improve relations with the United States and, in the absence of a strong Turkish-American population that could battle Ankara's main antagonists in Washington, the Greek and Armenian-American lobbies, he decided to actively pursue American-Jewish groups. He understood that for that to succeed, Ankara's relations with Israel had to also improve. These relations had reached a nadir in 1981, when the Turkish generals reduced diplomatic relations to the lowest possible level. Özal began to actively court Turkish Jews to lobby their coreligionists in America in Turkey's favor. Evolving ties with U.S. Jews, especially in Congress, provided Ankara with the means to balance its opponents, although the specter of an Armenian Genocide resolution being introduced on the floor of the House or Senate never fully disappeared.

---

*... the Israeli-Turkish relationship was never conceived as a bilateral one. Washington provided the incentive and glue for this emerging alliance.*

---

The more hopeful atmosphere created after the 1993 conclusion of the Oslo Agreements also helped improve relations. The major breakthrough came about with the signing of the 1996 Military Training and Cooperation Agreement, which was followed in turn by a free trade agreement, which came into force in 2000. Israel, as part of the military agreement, won a number of major contracts to refurbish aging Turkish military equipment as well as the right to train over Turkish airspace, a vital need given the narrowness of Israeli airspace. Similarly, Turkish pilots trained with their Israeli counterparts on a variety of systems.

The Turkish military, however, had domestic political calculations in mind when it signed the agreement with Israel. Although not at the top of its priorities, Turkish officers delighted in forcing Necmettin Erbakan, the first Islamist prime minister and an unabashed anti-Semite, into signing an agreement with Israel. (By doing so, they also planted the seeds of discontent with the agreement. Many members of the current Justice and Development Party (AKP), including the current Turkish president, Abdullah Gül, had been members of the Erbakan government or his party. The memory of his humiliation at the hands of the officers would not dissipate easily.) The most important weakness in the Turkish-Israeli agreement, however, was the lack of Turkish domestic support. Turkish public opinion had always been very pro-Palestinian, and despite the burgeoning economic ties with Israel and the added benefits of putting pressure on Syria, the Turkish public remained lukewarm. The brief exception was during the devastating 1999 Istanbul earthquake when Israeli rescue teams proved much more adept than their Turkish counterparts in saving lives, and thereby earned much admiration. In the end, this proved to be short-lived.

The putative alliance paid its most important dividend when Turkey told the Hafez al-Asad regime in 1998 to either kick PKK leader Öcalan out of Syria or hand him over to Turkey. The Syrians, and most importantly other Arab countries, were convinced that they were facing a pincer movement of sorts orchestrated by Israel and Turkey.[1] Fearing the worst, al-Asad capitulated.

Relations between Israel and Turkey began to deteriorate with the collapse of the Oslo process and the beginning of the Second Intifada (2000). Prime Minister Bülent Ecevit, of the center-left Democratic Left Party, accused Israel of committing "genocide" in Jenin following the bitter clashes in that town in the occupied West Bank. The irony of Turks accusing Israelis of genocide when they relied on American-Jewish groups to defend them from accusations of committing genocide against Armenians was not lost in Washington.

The AKP came to power in 2002, intent on demonstrating to all that it was a responsible political party and not an Islamist one. One of the first policy pronouncements the AKP made was to vouch for Turkey's EU vocation; as much as the AKP was serious about this goal, it was also an important message sent to different constituencies, from Washington to Europe to its domestic public. Almost immediately after winning elections, the AKP government found itself facing an impossible situation as the Bush administration was rapidly gearing up to invade Iraq. Despite its objections to the war, the AKP leadership decided to agree to allow the American 4th Infantry Brigade to traverse Turkish territory en route to opening a second front against Saddam Hussein. Although the parliamentary vote that ultimately denied the United States this chance may have been the result of the AKP's mismanagement and inexperience, the fact is that it created doubts about the party's real vision.

In this context, the AKP's relations with Israel would become a litmus test of the party's political tendencies. AKP leaders maintained cordial relations with Israel as trade relations blossomed and the AKP did not undo any existing contract or arms purchases from Israel. Turkey could, by having good relations with both sides in the Arab-Israeli conflict, claim that it was the only regional power capable of bridging the divide. In this

---

1. Ironically, the Israelis publicly announced that they were withdrawing forces from the Golan in order to demonstrate to the Syrians that they had no part in this. Moreover, the Turks had not moved any forces to the Syrian border despite rumors to the contrary.

vein, by initiating negotiations between Israel and Syria, Ankara received many accolades. On the other hand, the AKP's invitation to the hard-line, Damascus-based Hamas leader, Khaled Meshal, following that party's victory in the Palestinian elections in 2006, was criticized in the United States. Again, it seemed to Americans that Turkey was contradicting some of the basic tenets of its foreign policy: It was providing respectability to the militant organization that had been deemed by both Europe and the United States as a terrorist group, while continuously pushing for tougher measures on the PKK worldwide.

The Israelis swallowed hard and refrained from reacting too harshly to the Meshal invitation. At some level, they hoped that Ankara might, as it claimed it could, moderate Hamas's behavior. Still, occasional anti-Israeli outbursts by Erdoğan continued to trouble the relationship. Throughout this period, the AKP kept its eye on Washington and its reactions. Even Erdoğan's first trip to Israel in 2005—after numerous rejections—was interpreted as an attempt "to improve the climate of U.S.-Turkish relations."[2]

## The Crisis

The Israeli-Turkish relationship came apart with the Gaza War in late 2008-early 2009. It was both the timing and violence associated with Operation Cast Lead that caused the Turks to effectively jettison their ties to Israel. From then on, Erdoğan did not miss an opportunity to castigate and condemn Israel, often using extremely harsh language. Perhaps the most emblematic moment was the Davos incident, where on a public stage he admonished and tried to humiliate Israeli President Shimon Peres. Though his performance in Davos made him a hero in the proverbial Arab and Turkish streets, it alienated many in the United States who have tended to see Peres as someone who has pushed for a new, peaceful, and prosperous Middle East.

Davos was a defining moment in Turkey's relations with Israel, and as Erdoğan would later admit in an interview with a Spanish daily, *El Pais*, "Davos had become a principal founding block of Turkish foreign policy."[3] Davos also represented the beginning of a new Turkish approach that privileged opposition to Israel. Hence, on the Iranian nuclear question,

2. Alexander Murinson, "The Strategic Depth Doctrine of Turkish Foreign Policy," *Middle Eastern Studies*, Vol. 42, No. 6 (November 2006), p. 959.
3. Quoted in *HaberX*, February 22, 2010.

Erdoğan in particular questioned and underplayed Western concerns and instead chose to make Israel's nuclear arsenal the issue, while glossing over the crucial difference of Nuclear Non-Proliferation Treaty obligations and responsibilities. Iran, after all was a signatory country, and Israel was not. By the same token, Pakistan and India, who are in the same category as Israel, got a pass from Turkey. Erdoğan furthermore reiterated his view that suspicions of Iranian nuclear ambitions were nothing more than gossip; he was assured, he said, by the Iranian leadership that their program was peaceful.

*The flotilla debacle had a very direct impact on how the AKP was perceived in the United States, especially in the halls of Congress.*

Things would only get worse. On May 31, 2010, Israel intercepted a Gaza-bound Turkish ship with pro-Palestinian activists from a number of countries. In the resulting melee, eight Turks and one Turkish American were killed. This event sent the already deteriorating bilateral relations into a tailspin. As Turkey and Israel engaged in a war of words, Ankara recalled its ambassador and insisted on an apology and compensation from Israel as well as a complete lifting of the blockade on Gaza. Relations would have deteriorated further had it not been for the intercession of Washington. The Obama administration, which had assumed power just as the Gaza War ended, found itself in a difficult situation, besieged by both Turks and Israelis to choose sides in the flotilla confrontation. Although the facts surrounding the events remained murky, it was clear that the Israelis botched the raid and were unprepared for what was awaiting them, while the Turkish participants, who had unofficial backing from the AKP, were intent from the start to trigger a confrontation.

The flotilla debacle had a very direct impact on how the AKP was perceived in the United States, especially in the halls of Congress. Many on Capitol Hill were already upset at the way Erdoğan had been lambasting the Israelis. The flotilla crisis came on the heels of the Brazilian-Turkish-Iranian deal on the Tehran Research Reactor that was rejected by Washington and its allies and the subsequent no vote by Ankara at the UN Security Council on expanding sanctions on the Islamic Republic. It is perhaps this divergence over Iran that has done the most to cloud perceptions of Turkey in Washington. The fact that Turkey as a NATO member would break with alliance partners, fashion a separate deal, and even cross two countries that hitherto had been reluctant players in the Iranian saga, China and Russia, surprised many in Congress.

Part of the problem lies in Washington in that it has failed to keep pace with the rapid changes in Turkey and consequently with Turkish foreign policy. Turkey's ambitions, buoyed by its economic and political successes, to become an important regional if not global power, its hubris in thinking that it could impose its vision on its neighbors, and most importantly, the growing importance of expanding commercial linkages have dramatically changed the Turkish government's behavior. Ankara was seen in Washington, however, as having gone too far, providing succor to Iranian attempts at deceiving the international community and in the process failing to support its principal ally.

The general confrontation with Israel, though long in the making, the controversy of the nuclear issue, and the flotilla episode helped forge in the minds of many that Turkey, under a mildly Islamist government, was veering out of the Western orbit and was maybe more interested in "Muslim" and Middle Eastern concerns overall than in alliance commitments. Even among observers in the United States and Europe who did not subscribe to the theory of "the rise of an Islamist Turkey under the AKP's tutelage," Turkish foreign policy evoked puzzlement and even anxiety regarding Ankara's commitment to its Western vocations. Some even argued that it was the European Union that was at fault because, especially with the rise of President Nicolas Sarkozy in France and Chancellor Angela Merkel in Germany, the European message had been much less welcoming of Turkey and was, therefore, pushing the Turks away from the European Union and the West in general.

## American Domestic Politics and the Turkish Imagination

The Obama administration, which included Turkey in the president's first European trip, clearly hoped for a new type of partnership with Ankara. The AKP had made the best of the weakening American position in the Middle East following the Iraq War by embarking on a whirlwind of diplomatic, political, and economic initiatives in the region. Whereas relations with Israel frayed, Ankara turned its Iraq policy on its head and engaged the Kurdish Regional Government, which it had shunned and had tried to undermine in the past. Turkey emerged as an important partner in Iraq, whereas it had previously been obstructionist. The AKP government also broke with traditional recalcitrant policies in Cyprus, instituting approaches that were far more accommodating of a solution on the divided island.

That said, one of the administration's greatest disappointments with Turkey was in the Caucasus. Secretary of State Hillary Clinton and her team actively encouraged and negotiated a set of protocols designed to open the Armenian-Turkish border and begin a process of normalization between the two countries. Ankara was clearly motivated by the prospect of a potential Armenian Genocide resolution on Capitol Hill as well as a statement by President Obama, who as a senator had strongly urged his fellow legislators to recognize the Armenian Genocide as a historical fact. Once President Obama issued a proclamation on April 24, 2009, recognizing the massacres of 1915 (without the genocide word being uttered), Turkish support for the protocols disappeared. Holding the proverbial bag, the State Department leadership was embarrassed for having sold the idea to the White House and, in the process, it alienated large numbers of Armenian-American voters who had hoped that they finally had in Obama a president who would acknowledge the genocide.

The Turkish strategy until recently had relied on American Jews for support on critical issues, such as the Armenian Genocide and Cyprus. Ankara's change on Cyprus, even if unsuccessful in the medium term, reduced the need for support on this issue from American Jews. The Turks, ironically, have always overestimated and misunderstood the role of the "Jewish lobby." The AKP has also reduced much of the complexity of American politics and foreign policy to two elements, Israel and Jewish influence in the United States and the world.[4]

Even when relations with Israel and with American Jewish groups were running smoothly, many members of Congress of Jewish origin were very supportive of Armenian claims. In part, this was easily

---

4. Erdoğan has often talked about the influence of Jews in the media. A senior Turkish foreign ministry official, commenting to the author on the Turkey-Brazil gambit, argued that Erdoğan and Davutoğlu perceived the Obama administration's opposition to Iran's nuclear program as a result of Israeli and Jewish pressure. He admitted that there was little consideration given to American concerns on proliferation, the administration's wider goals regarding nuclear arms reduction, or the ratification of agreements with Russia.

explained by their representation of districts, mostly in California, where Armenian Americans held considerable political sway. Ironically, if Armenian Americans expected that the "Jewish lobby" would swing to their side following Erdoğan's diatribes against Israel, they were wrong. In fall 2009, when the Armenian Genocide resolution was voted in the House Foreign Relations Committee, it passed with the barest of majorities, 23-22.[5]

The flotilla incident has, of course, inflamed passions further. A great deal more criticism of Turkey has been emanating from institutions either Jewish in origin or associated with Jewish causes since the unfolding of those unfortunate events. The U.S. Senate passed a resolution strongly supporting Israel's right to self-defense in this case. Still, there was no discernible campaign against Turkey. There was an element of perhaps wishful thinking that somehow these two allies would find a way to fix their relations. The Obama administration did not shy away from interacting and consulting with Erdoğan, as was evidenced during the crises over the departure of President Hosni Mubarak in Egypt and over the events in Syria. In fact, much of the general criticism directed at Turkey has had to do with Iran as much as it has had to do with Israel. Erdoğan's rhetoric has not helped either, as when he said, "Some saw the Star of David and the Nazi swastika in the same light."[6] Turks, even those quite familiar with American politics, have been quick to blame a sinister Jewish cabal behind criticisms of the AKP government, even when their criticisms were directed at Turkish efforts to curtail press freedoms.[7]

---

5. The votes in favor of the resolution in 2009 were fewer than earlier attempts; there also was no evidence suggesting that Jewish groups had decided to punish the Turks for their break with Israel. This did not stop Erdoğan from monitoring "the voting patterns of Jewish members of that committee," (private communication). Congress's sole Muslim member, Keith Ellison, also voted in favor of the Armenians and against Turkey.
6. Sedat Ergin, "Nazizimle Yahudiliğin Sembolleri Bir Tutulabilir Mi?" *Hürriyet*, June 16, 2010.
7. Cengiz Çandar, "Polis devleti' söyleminin kaynağı ya da Türkiye karşıtı tsunami," *Radikal*, March 15, 2011. When the venerable English weekly *The Economist*, in a lead editorial, called on Turks to strengthen the opposition against the AKP in the June 12, 2011 elections, Besir Atatlay, the former interior minister, claimed that this was a plot by the Israeli lobby. See Amberin Zaman, "Egemen Bagis'i yeni gorevine davet ediyorum," *Habertürk*, June 7, 2011.

## Prospects

For both Israel and Turkey, the post–flotilla crisis stakes are high. Earlier, the crisis was over disagreements about policies concerning third parties. This time, because each side perceives the action of the other as against its own interests, it will be much more difficult to circumvent the obstacles. Moreover, each side has not only lost confidence in the other, but is also overwhelmed by a sense of betrayal. Hence, even if there were to be some resolution of the flotilla problem, Israel and Turkey are sufficiently alienated from each other that the chances of a return to amicable relations, much less a quasi-alliance, are virtually nonexistent in the medium term. In both countries, domestic politics plays a significant role. Turkey did not veto Israel's admission into the OECD in 2010 despite the two countries' quarrels. Had it done so, it would have triggered a backlash in the United States. Yet, it is difficult to see how Turkey could not have vetoed such a membership prospect if the vote had taken place after the flotilla crisis.

Moreover, the Turks feel vindicated by their stand on both Israel and Gaza. Hence, they have few incentives to seek a change in either the relationship or reducing the level of acrimony that has characterized their rhetoric. More fundamentally, Erdoğan and his party were always motivated by a desire to transform relations with the United States and free Turkey from perceived dependency on relations with Israel and reliance on Jewish groups for support in Washington. The AKP sees Turkey as a far more important country in the region than Israel given its economic prowess, its cultural and historical ties to many regional countries, and its increasing soft power. Hence, it sees itself in competition with Israel not just in the region, but also in Washington. But Israel, with its special relationship with the United States, reminds the Turks that they cannot be *primus inter pares*. As Soli Özel has argued, part of the problem between Turkey and Israel is structural:

> Turkey increasingly sees itself as a regional power and seeks to be America's main partner in the region. Under the rubric of 'model partnership' introduced by President Obama, Ankara believes that it has a chance to forge such a relation that will inevitably come at the expense of Israel's most-favored and protected status.[8]

---

8. Soli Özel, "The Future of Turkey and Israel," *World Affairs Journal*, July 1, 2010. http://www.worldaffairsjournal.org/new/blogs/ozel/date/2010/7/1.

The Arab Spring has turned Turkey's foreign policy calculations upside down. Mum on Tunisia, Erdoğan publicly called on Mubarak to leave office—but it was clear by then that the Egyptian leader had lost his army's and Washington's confidence. The irony is that Turkey has become a status quo power in the region, perhaps not too different from the United States; it has established close ties to many regimes and has also to worry about sizable business interests and investments.

Its foreign policy constraints as originally demonstrated in the Libyan crisis hurt Turkey's reputation in Washington. In the case of Libya, Erdoğan was initially reluctant to break with Qaddafi, objected to the imposition of sanctions, even those that targeted the regime, on the grounds that it would hurt the average Libyan, and indicated that he would not support a NATO-imposed no-fly zone. In Libya, Turkish firms had billions of dollars invested, primarily in the construction sector, and thousands of Turkish workers made a living there. Even after a UN Security Council vote, Turkey opposed military action against the Libyan regime. This is reminiscent of Ankara's stand after the disputed election results in Iran: Turkey was one of the first to congratulate President Mahmoud Ahmedinejad for his electoral victory in June 2009. President Gül had the unfortunate occasion to recently visit Tehran on the day when democracy activists had taken to the streets, only to be violently beaten back by the security forces. Yet Gül, other than making an oblique reference to regimes in the region heeding their populations, was silent. On Libya, the Turks were ultimately forced to execute a 180-degree reversal. Qaddafi could no longer be defended, and Ankara publicly called on him to step down.

The next test case for Turkey turned out to be its immediate neighbor to the south, Syria, where the AKP government had woven a set of close relationships with the Bashar al-Asad regime. A free trade agreement, a no-visa policy, and a push for joint cabinet meetings under the rubric of "two nations, one government" have come to naught with Damascus. There too, after trying to offer advice to Bashar, whom Erdoğan had come to view as his younger brother, Turkey found that it could not keep silent on the regime's carnage. The stream of refugees crossing into Turkish territory made it impossible to ignore the violence. This time, however, the Turks acted faster and have closely coordinated with the White House.

Amidst this rapprochement with Washington, the Turks have at least yielded to one request from the Americans. They pulled back their support for another flotilla that had been scheduled in June 2011, thereby removing a major irritant from the U.S.-Turkish bilateral dialogue. Although this does not mean that Turkish-Israeli relations are set to return to their halcyon days, it does open up the opportunity for a negotiated outcome—though internal Israeli politics makes this still hard to achieve.

All these factors are likely to play a role in Washington's perceptions of Ankara. Despite its significance, Israel is hardly the only issue that drives discourse and ideas on Turkey among leaders and policymakers in the United States. As the role and importance of Turkey increases in the region, a myriad of factors will continue to influence Washington's relations with Turkey.

7

# Turkey's Relations with the United States and Israel under the Justice and Development Party Government

*Yaprak Gürsoy, Bilgi University, Istanbul*

The Justice and Development Party (AKP) has been in power in Turkey since the 2002 elections. The rise of the AKP to power coincided with fundamental changes in Turkish foreign policy, especially in the Middle East. Since the early 2000s, Turkish foreign policy has been geared toward its eastern neighbors more than its traditional Western allies. Turkey has cordial, if not friendly, relations with countries that the West considers as rogue states, such as Iran and Syria, and its partnership with the United States and Israel has been unraveling. Turkish foreign policy, which was centered on the "Turkey–United States–Israel triangle" in the 1990s,[1] does not rely on these two allies anymore.

How much of this transformation is due to the AKP and its ideological convictions? Turkish foreign policy analysts and observers, who are skeptical of the AKP's commitment to democracy and to Turkey's secular state tradition, point out that the party is a byproduct of the National Outlook

1. Ziya Öniş and Şuhnaz Yılmaz, "Between Europeanization and Euro-Asianism: Foreign Policy Activism in Turkey during the AKP Era," *Turkish Studies*, Vol.10, No.1 (March 2009), p.17.

(*Milli Görüş*) movement. Since the 1970s, the National Outlook has been the most significant religion-based political movement in Turkey. The political party of the movement, the Welfare Party, held power between 1996 and 1997 as the lead partner of a coalition government. The ideology of the National Outlook and the election manifesto of the Welfare Party in the 1990s were explicitly against the West and Israel. The movement did not recognize the State of Israel and blamed Westernization as the cause of Turkey's economic problems.[2] The Welfare Party advocated cooperating with the Muslim states of the Middle East in order to counteract the power and influence of Europe and the United States. Zionism was seen as the "local manifestation of Western hegemony,"[3] and therefore, it had to be confronted with the cooperation of Islamic nations.

In February 1997, the Welfare Party and its coalition partner were forced to resign due to the pressure of the secular Turkish military. After the Constitutional Court closed the party and its heir, the movement split into two different factions. The younger members of the Welfare Party founded the AKP, with a more moderate program than its predecessor. Even though the AKP's program and election manifestos do not contain anti-Semitic or anti-Western elements, the fact that the leaders of the

---

*There is reason to believe that the essentials of Turkish foreign policy would have been the same in the last decade if Turkey had been ruled by a more secular political party.*

---

party were members of the more radical Welfare Party has increased suspicions at home and abroad that the AKP has not abandoned its Islamic roots. The policies of the party toward the Middle East and the West provide further evidence to skeptics that Turkish foreign policy has been "Islamized" under the rule of the AKP.

---

2. Tarık Oğuzlu, "The Changing Dynamics of Turkey-Israel Relations: A Structural Realist Account," *Mediterranean Politics*, Vol. 15, No. 2 (July 2010), p. 276.

3. The party failed to carry out these foreign policy objectives during its short term in office. Hasret Dikici Bilgin, "Foreign Policy Orientation of Turkey's Pro-Islamist Parties: A Comparative Study of the AKP and Refah," *Turkish Studies*, Vol. 9, No. 3 (September 2008), p. 408-409.

Despite the change in Turkish foreign policy under the rule of the AKP, this paper will argue that this transformation is not due primarily to the Justice and Development Party and its ideological roots. Undoubtedly the goals and perspectives of the AKP leaders explain important elements of the new foreign policy and especially the desire to increase Turkey's cooperation with its neighbors. However, there is reason to believe that the essentials of Turkish foreign policy would have been the same in the last decade if Turkey had been ruled by a more secular political party. Relations with the West and Israel had started to deteriorate in the late 1990s, before the AKP came to power and when a more secular coalition government was in power. During its first term in office the AKP tried to ease tensions and attempted to establish good relations with Israel. The party also adopted a pro-EU and pro-Western stance, as its policies have never been consistently anti-Western. It seems that the party goes back and forth in its emphasis on anti-American and anti-Israeli rhetoric depending on the stance of the public. The Turkish electorate has grown increasingly conservative and anti-American in the last decade, and public opinion is overwhelmingly supportive of the Palestinian cause. The attitudes of the opposition parties and the media have had serious consequences in shaping the policies of the AKP, leading to a vicious circle in which the government's outbursts against the United States and Israel shape public opinion even more against Turkey's traditional allies.

## A Synopsis of Turkey's Relations with its Middle Eastern Neighbors, the United States, and Israel

Any assessment of Turkish foreign policy toward the United States and Israel should take into account the country's relations with its eastern neighbors, especially Iran and Syria. In the 1990s, Turkey cooperated with Israel due to perceived threats from its Middle Eastern neighbors. In the last decade, these perceptions gradually changed, in part as a result of the war in Iraq. New circumstances in the region forced Turkey, Syria, and Iran to alter their strategies toward one another. In the 1990s, Syria and Iran lent support to the Kurdish separatist movement in Turkey. However, after the war in Iraq, the two neighbors of Baghdad began to cooperate with Ankara against the possibility of an independent Kurdish state in the region.

As relations with these countries improved, Washington started to question Turkey's commitment to the Western alliance. The ultimate aim of Turkey and the United States remains the same with regard to Syria and Iran. Ankara, like Washington, wants these countries to be stable democracies. However, as Tarık Oğuzlu has argued, "For Ankara, the only way to bring regime change in Iran and Syria is to open the channels of communications with the leadership in these countries," and incorporate them "into the globalized world."[4] Similarly, Turkey is as much threatened by the prospect of Iran acquiring nuclear weapons as Western nations. However, contrary to the United States and its allies, Turkey is confident that this question can be resolved through diplomatic means. For this purpose, Turkey made an attempt to promote international dialogue with Iran. In May 2010, Turkey and Brazil arranged a fuel swap agreement with Iran, which would exchange Iran's low-enriched uranium with 20-percent enriched fuel to be used only for non-military purposes. After the agreement failed to meet the approval of European states and the American administration, Turkey voted against applying new sanctions against Iran in the United Nations Security Council.

Turkish foreign policy toward Iran is guided also by economic relations, as evidenced by the convening of the Turkish-Iranian Business Forum as part of President Abdullah Gül's visit to Tehran in February 2011.[5] Between 1999 and 2009, the volume of trade between Iran and Turkey increased from $350 million to $10 billion. Although Turkey imports oil and gas from Tehran, Turkish companies, specialized in textiles, food, and chemicals, have invested at least $1 billion worth of assets in the country.[6]

Turkey's relations with Syria, another southeastern neighbor, have been similarly positive. Since the signing of the 2002 military training agreement, the two countries have cooperated in strategic matters. In 2004, Turkey and Syria signed a free trade agreement, and in 2009 they abolished their visa regimes to facilitate economic cooperation. The volume of trade between the two countries increased from $530 million in 1995 to $2 billion in 2009.[7] It was expected that trade volume would

---

4. Tarık Oğuzlu, "Middle Easternization of Turkey's Foreign Policy: Does Turkey Dissociate from the West?" *Turkish Studies*, Vol. 9, No. 1 (March 2008), p. 9.
5. Sercan Doğan, "Cumhurbaşkanı Abdullah Gül'ün İran Ziyareti: Arka Plan ve Beklentiler," *Ortadoğu Stratejik Araştırmalar Merkezi* (ORSAM) Diş Politika Analizleri, http://www.orsam.org.tr/tr/yazigoster.aspx?ID=1495 (accessed March 5, 2011).
6. Mustafa Kutluay, "Is Turkey Drifting Away from the West? An Economic Interpretation (1/2)," *Journal of Turkish Weekly*, October 28, 2009.
7. Kemal Kirişçi, "Turkey's Foreign Policy in Turbulent Times," Chaillot Paper, No. 92, (September 2006), p.107; Bülent Aras, "Turkey between Syria and Israel: Turkey's Rising Soft Power," SETA Foundation for Political, Economic and Social Research, Policy Brief No. 15, (2008), p.2.

further increase to $5 billion in the subsequent three years.[8] State officials from both countries made frequent visits to their counterparts and, suggestively, in January 2011, the Turkish Prime Minister Recep Tayyip Erdoğan and Syrian Prime Minister Muhammad Naji al-Otari together launched the building of the "Friendship Dam" on the Orontes River.

Such policies of Turkey toward Iran and Syria led to concern in Washington and European capitals. Turkey seemed to have turned its back on the European Union, especially after the European Union's 2006 decision to freeze parts of Turkish accession talks. F. Stephen Larrabee has judged that since the end of the Cold War, and increasingly in the last decade, Washington and Ankara "have lost their agreed sense of common strategic purpose. The result has been an increasing decoupling of U.S. and Turkish strategic interests."[9] This rift became apparent in March 2003, when the Turkish Parliament voted against the use of Turkish territory for the deployment of U.S. troops during the Second Gulf War. After the start of the war in March 2003, the humiliating detention of eleven Turkish soldiers in northern Iraq by Americans exposed the fact that the Turkish-U.S. partnership in the region cannot always be based on mutual interests. Even though the Obama administration initially attempted to revive relations by describing them as a "model partnership," Ankara's unilateral attempts to engage in dialogue with Iran, its vote against UN sanctions, and cooperation with Syria have led to disappointment and doubts in Washington about the viability of the alliance.

Another cause for concern for the United States has been Turkey's increasingly problematic relations with Israel. It appears that as Turkey reconciled relations with its southeastern neighbors, it has also abandoned its traditional ally in the Middle East. During the AKP's term in office, one of the first instances of deteriorating relations between the two countries was the reaction of Turkey to Israel's Operation Cast Lead in Gaza in late 2008 to early 2009. Prime Minister Erdoğan and President Shimon Peres quarreled over the issue in public in January 2009 at the World Economic Forum in Davos. The second major incident that marked the crisis between the two countries was the Israeli military raid on the flotilla carrying aid to Gaza on May 31, 2010. The attack, which took place

8. "Suriye'yle ticaret hacmini 5 milyar $'a çıkaracağız," *Dünya Gazetesi*, July 23, 2009, www.dunyagazetesi.com.tr (accessed June 10, 2010).
9. F. Stephen Larrabee, "The 'New Turkey' and American-Turkish Relations," *Insight Turkey*, Vol. 13, No. 1 (Winter 2011), p. 5.

in international waters, killed eight Turkish civilians and one Turkish-American. For the first time since the Republic of Turkey was founded, Turkish civilians were killed by the armed forces of a foreign nation. In fact, Foreign Minister Ahmet Davutoğlu remarked on the significance of the incident for Turkey by equating it with September 11. Shortly after the episode, officials in Ankara declared that Turkish-Israeli relations would never be the same and that the death of civilians in the hands of the Israeli military would never be forgotten.[10] Even though Washington has been pressuring Ankara to reconcile with Israel, it seems that the two Middle Eastern partners will not reach their previous levels of cooperation in the near future.

There is no doubt that Turkish foreign policy has entered into a new era under the rule of the AKP. The clear-cut choice of the government to seek good relations with Syria and Iran and its pro-Palestinian attitudes put a strain on Turkey's partnership with the United States and Israel. However, the question remains: How many of these changes are due to the AKP's ideological stance? The remainder of the paper will try to provide an answer to this question, first by outlining the main elements of the AKP's foreign policy and then by elucidating the domestic causes of changing relations with Israel and the United States.

## AKP Foreign Policy in the Middle East

The policies of the AKP in the Middle East and other neighboring areas rely on the strategy of making Turkey a central and leading country in the region. The AKP hopes to achieve this position by assuming two interrelated roles. The first is the role of an arbitrator of conflict in the region, and the second is the role of a model for Muslim countries. While such self-identified functions require Turkey to have good relations or "zero problems with neighbors," both positions are also closely related to Turkey's alliance with Israel and the United States.

Turkey's ambition to be a broker and arbitrator particularly requires the acquiescence and willingness of Israel. For the purpose of bringing peace to the Middle East, the AKP government has attempted to facilitate dialogue between Israeli and Palestinian officials. In May 2005, during his visit to Israel, Prime Minister Erdoğan sought to understand how Turkey

---

10. Gencer Özcan, "Aynalar Galerisi: Türkiye-İsrail İlişkilerinde Yansımalar, Yanılsamalar ve Gerçekler," Ortadoğu Analiz, Vol. 2, No. 18 (June 2010), p. 37.

could contribute to regional peace. His efforts paid off when in September 2005, Turkey brought the foreign ministers of Israel and Palestine together in Istanbul.[11] Subsequently, in February 2006, Turkey invited the leader of Hamas, Khaled Meshal, to Ankara and informed Israel about the talks. A year later, Prime Minister Ehud Olmert, during his visit to Turkey, declared that if Hamas accepted some conditions, Israel would be willing to talk with the organization in a meeting conducted under the auspices of Turkey.[12]

The AKP made similar efforts to negotiate peace between Israel and Syria. One of the most successful episodes in this process took place in May 2008, when indirect talks between the two countries' officials were carried out in Turkey. Indeed, Turkey's strong condemnation of Operation Cast Lead, the suspension of the Turkish effort to mediate between Syria and Israel, and the subsequent worsening of relations between Turkey and Israel all stemmed in good part from the feeling of betrayal that the AKP leadership felt as a result of a conviction that Olmert had used the negotiations as a cover for his Gaza plans. Just one week before the Israeli operation started in December 2008, Olmert visited Ankara, which almost led to a meeting between him and Syrian Foreign Minister Walid al-Muallam. Erdoğan personally took offense that during the visit the Israeli prime minister did not inform him of the upcoming military campaign and give his word that there would be "no humanitarian tragedy . . . in Gaza."[13] Ankara lost credibility as a mediator in Syria and Palestine after Operation Cast Lead, and the government's efforts and hopes were shattered. This frustration ultimately led to Erdoğan's quarrel with Peres in Davos and the subsequent downward spiraling of relations.

The second role that the AKP aims at—the position of an exemplar for the other Middle Eastern nations—is closely related to U.S. policies in the region. Since the end of the Cold War and increasingly after the events of September 11, American administrations have portrayed Turkey as a role model in the Middle East. Since Turkey is a Muslim country with a stable democratic regime and Western and secular traditions, Washington perceived Turkey as a model that would balance the possible leadership

---

11. İlker Aytürk, "Between Crises and Cooperation: The Future of Turkish-Israeli Relations," *Insight Turkey*, Vol. 11, No. 2 (2009), p. 60.
12. Özcan, "Aynalar Galerisi," p. 41.
13. Quoted in Selin M. Bölme, "Charting Turkish Diplomacy in the Gaza Conflict," *Insight Turkey*, Vol. 11, No. 1 (2009), p. 24.

of Iran. The Greater Middle East initiative of the Bush administration, U.S. democratization efforts in the region, and Turkey's elected and moderately Islamist government in power combined to establish Turkey as a role model.

Even though the AKP leadership also believes that Turkey can set an example in its neighborhood, the party thinks that such a role can be achieved only if Turkey assumes a leadership position as well. Such leadership, however, translates into the AKP government engaging in dialogue with authoritarian leaders in the Middle East and assuming an increasingly populist (meaning anti-Western, anti-Israeli, and pro-Palestinian) rhetoric. In addition to cooperating with the regimes of Syria, Iran, and Sudan, Prime Minister Erdoğan accepted the Al-Qaddafi International Prize for Human Rights in November 2010. After the protests and revolts in Libya, Erdoğan was criticized at home for not returning the prize, but he argued that the prize was for his efforts in Palestine, and therefore, he had no intention of handing it back.[14]

On the pro-democracy protests in the Arab world, Erdoğan criticized the European Union for not taking a stance and accused the West of prioritizing their oil interests over democratization in North Africa. During his trip to Germany, the prime minister argued against applying sanctions and carrying out a NATO operation in Libya. In a typical populist and anti-Western speech, Erdoğan declared: "Tunisia belongs to the Tunisian people, Egypt belongs to the Egyptian people. They determine their own fates."[15] In an earlier announcement that provided support to the Egyptian protestors, Erdoğan used Islamic symbols to warn Egyptian president Hosni Mubarak: "All of us will die and will be questioned over what we left behind . . . . As Muslims, where we all go is a two cubic meter hole."[16]

The AKP government sees in the recent protests a new opportunity for Turkey to become a role model for the region with its democracy and burgeoning economy. However, Erdoğan increasingly uses anti-Westernism and Islam as tools to increase his popularity. Certainly, this is not the type of model that the United States has envisioned for Turkey, and using such a discourse in the name of promoting democracy in the region puts an

14. "O Ödül Filistin İçin," *Hürriyet*, February 23, 2011, p. 22.
15. "NATO'nun Libya'da Ne İşi Var?" *Hürriyet*, March 1, 2011, p. 21.
16. "Turkey tells Mubarak to listen to the people," *Reuters*, February 1, 2011. http://www.reuters.com/article/2011/02/01/us-egypt-turkey-idUSTRE71047Y20110201 (accessed March 08, 2011).

increasing strain on the Turkish-American partnership. There is no doubt that some aspects of Turkish foreign policy, such as having no problems with neighbors, mediating peace in the Middle East, and becoming a paragon of democracy among Muslim countries have influenced Turkey's relations with the United States and Israel.

Although the leadership position Turkey seeks is somewhat unique to the AKP, two important points should not be forgotten. First, there is nothing that is anti-Western or pro-Islam at the core of the AKP's doctrine—despite the fact that the prime minister increasingly uses such rhetoric to realize the party's goals. As compared with the Welfare Party and the National Outlook ideology of the 1990s, the AKP's pro-EU stance has been quite remarkable. In fact, during its first term in office, the AKP carried out major EU accession reforms in domestic politics, which led Ofra Bengio to describe one of the policies of the AKP government as "attempting to strike a new balance between its European and Middle Eastern policies."[17]

---

*The AKP's course of action has not been consistently anti-Israeli.*

---

Even though the AKP seems to have abandoned its goal of EU membership since 2007, the party has not been consistently anti-Western. It seems that AKP policy is more inconsistent and ambiguous than well defined. Some of the rhetoric of the party leadership is for the domestic audience, which has become increasingly anti-American and anti-Israeli since the early 2000s—before the AKP even came to power. This is the second important point that will be analyzed in detail below.

## Old Wine in New Bottles: Ambiguities in Turkish Foreign Policy since the Early 2000s

Even though Turkey and Israel were allies and cooperated militarily in the 1990s, their relations were put to test in the early 2000s. The coalition government of the Democratic Left (DSP), National Action (MHP), and Motherland (ANAP) parties came to power in 1999 and ruled the country

17. Ofra Bengio, "Altercating Interests and Orientations between Israel and Turkey: A View from Israel," *Insight Turkey*, Vol. 11, No. 2 (2009), p. 44.

until the victory of the AKP in the November 2002 elections. During its three years in government, the DSP-MHP-ANAP coalition had a cautious, yet ambiguous stance on Israel. It was the coalition government that initiated attempts to pursue good relations with neighbors, including Syria and Iran, as well as efforts to mediate regional conflicts through active use of diplomacy. Indeed, the early signs of what would happen in the subsequent years were clearly visible before the AKP came to power, and in some respects the party was merely continuing the policies of its predecessor.

The critical event that challenged Turkish-Israeli cooperation was the start of the Second Intifada in September 2000. As the Middle East peace process broke down in that period, Turkey tried to find a balance between Palestine and Israel, criticizing the former's terrorist activities, but at the same time sympathizing with their cause. In October 2000, along with several other Muslim countries, Turkey voted in favor of a draft resolution in the UN General Assembly that condemned Israel and envisioned the establishment of a mechanism that would investigate the events. The start of the Al-Aqsa Intifada also marked one of the first attempts of Turkey to actively pursue peace in the Middle East through international and regional organizations, such as the Organization of the Islamic Conference.[18]

The same official stance toward conflict in the region continued after Israel started Operation Defensive Shield in 2002, but this time government officials took a tougher line against Tel Aviv. Israel's use of force was criticized as excessive and violent, and the imposition of a siege on Yasser Arafat's compound was deemed "disrespectful." Foreign Minister Ismail Cem argued that the operation was against human rights and Prime Minister Bülent Ecevit went as far as describing Israel's attack on the Jenin camp as "genocide."[19] Despite these unprecedented outbursts, the official state policy continued to position itself between the two sides. In a joint declaration prepared by the offices of the president, general staff, and the prime minister, Turkey condemned both Israel's excessive use of force and the use of terrorism by the Palestinians. The same declaration also urged the United States to take more responsibility in the Middle East as a neutral arbitrator.

---

18. Özcan, "Aynalar Galerisi," p. 40.
19. Gencer Özcan, "Türkiye İsrail Yakınlaşmasında İlk Onyılın Ardından," in Mustafa Aydın and Çağrı Erhan (eds.), *Beş Deniz Havzasında Türkiye* (Ankara: Siyasal Kitapevi, 2006), pp. 337-339.

After the AKP came to power in 2002, Turkish foreign policy toward Israel and Palestine continued to be characterized by contradictory motives that left ambiguities unresolved. The main characteristics of Turkey's relations with Israel under the rule of the AKP can be described as follows:

- Trying to maintain and expand the military and political alliance between Turkey and Israel;
- Advocating a multilateral approach to solve the Israeli-Palestinian conflict;
- And harshly criticizing Israel at times, but backing down at other times, in order to uphold an appearance of neutrality and to maintain the above mentioned goals.

The first years of the AKP government witnessed efforts to expand the partnership between Turkey and Israel. Indeed, the program of the new government stated that this was a foreign policy goal. Accordingly, high-profile visits between state officials took place and the two countries signed an agreement to fight organized crime. However, relations deteriorated once again in 2004, when an Israeli offensive in Palestine began, and they got worse after the May attack against the Rafah refugee camp. Turkish government officials criticized Tel Aviv in quite harsh words. Prime Minister Erdoğan declared that the operation was "inhumane" and that Israel was carrying out "state terror." Foreign Minister Abdullah Gül, on the other hand, declared that Israel's behavior was "unsettling" and "unacceptable." After the death of two Hamas leaders in March and April 2004, the Ministry of Foreign Affairs accused Israel of carrying out "illegal assassinations."[20]

Despite these harsh declarations, the AKP government tried to resolve the conflict between Israel and Palestine by utilizing multilateral channels. There were calls to the United Nations and to the international community to go beyond merely condemning Israel. To that end, Turkey voted for a UN resolution to forward the issue of Israel's construction of a separation barrier along the West Bank to the International Court of Justice. The policy of the AKP government in 2004 was to carefully balance its criticism of Israel with such multilateral propositions, instead of strict measures, such as suspending bilateral relations with Israel.

20. Ibid., pp. 348-350.

Moreover, after their one-sided comments against Israel, government officials, including Erdoğan and Gül, issued follow-up statements that were much softer and included disapproval of suicide bombings and terrorist activities of the Palestinians. This kind of zigzagging foreign policy is evident from Erdoğan's decision in August 2004 to send his aides to Tel Aviv to smooth relations. The urging of the American administration and the personal request of President George W. Bush to mend relations with Israel partially explain this U-turn. To the satisfaction of Washington, by September 2004, the meetings in Israel had worked to stabilize relations between the two countries.

Turkish-Israeli relations deteriorated worse after the start of the AKP's second term in office, but the same policy characteristics and overall ambiguity have continued. The United States also still tries to maintain cooperation between its two allies in the Middle East. Immediately after the Davos incident, for instance, Israel and Turkey began "a new process of damage control and stabilization in diplomatic contacts."[21] In March 2009, Foreign Ministers Ali Babacan and Tzipi Livni met to reconcile the two countries' differences. Shortly before the Israeli raid on the aid flotilla in May 2010, Turkey renewed its efforts to mediate between Tel Aviv and Damascus, supported Israel's membership in the OECD, and scheduled a meeting between Foreign Minister Davutoğlu and Prime Minister Netanyahu in Washington. Even after the flotilla crisis, Turkey attempted to use multilateral channels and international organizations to resolve the conflict. The American administration played a critical role in persuading Israel to participate in the UN commission responsible for investigating the events. U.S. efforts to avoid an escalating crisis have succeeded in bringing government officials of the two countries together in Brussels. It is telling that just two months after the incident, Israel delivered four unmanned aerial vehicles, which Turkey uses in its combat against Kurdish separatists.

The AKP's course of action has not been consistently anti-Israeli. Turkish foreign policy since the late 1990s has fluctuated between close cooperation with Tel Aviv and harsh criticisms that threaten to sever ties completely. But such a breaking point in diplomatic contacts has never taken place, either before or after the AKP came to power. Ankara has cooperated with Israel in military and intelligence matters and has continued to purchase weapons from its defense industry. Therefore, the

21. Aytürk, "Between Crises and Cooperation," p. 67.

argument that the current crisis in relations is due solely to the AKP and its Islamic roots is an unwarranted assumption. Turkey and Israel share common threats, such as Iran, and they do not pose any strategic challenges to each other. Ankara cannot afford to lose its partnership with the United States completely, and the government is aware that Washington is closely monitoring the situation. Finally, the leadership role that the AKP wants Turkey to play in the region depends ultimately on the cooperation of Israel and the United States. For these reasons, the AKP government, regardless of its ideological convictions, cannot risk cutting off its diplomatic ties and military cooperation with Israel.

## Domestic Politics, Conservatism, and Nationalism in Turkey

If Turkish governments cannot afford to alienate Israel and the United States completely, why does the AKP increasingly use anti-American and anti-Israeli rhetoric? Although part of the explanation lies in the desire of the AKP to use populism as a tool to secure its leadership position in the Middle East, another cause is current public opinion in Turkey, which is characterized by conservatism, nationalism, and anti-Westernism.

When it comes to the Israeli-Palestinian conflict, all political parties in Turkey side with the latter and advocate taking action against Tel Aviv. This issue is one of the rare matters in Turkey that has the potential of uniting (at least at the discursive level) all political parties. It is important to note that the government's declarations against Israel in Davos and after the flotilla raid were not criticized by opposition parties. Similarly, before the June 2011 elections, the opposition parties seldom if ever commented on the AKP's foreign policy. One notable exception was the comment of the secularist Republican People's Party (CHP) leader Kemal Kılıçdaroğlu, during an overseas trip, that if his party were in government they would not have allowed *Mavi Marmara* to leave Turkish waters. During the same speech, Kılıçdaroğlu criticized the AKP's policy toward Israel and argued that both Israel and Turkey must take steps to normalize relations.[22] Despite this one incident, however, the main opposition party did not touch upon foreign policy issues frequently during the campaign. In a country where political parties usually use every opportunity to castigate each other, such unanimity is quite

22. "Kılıçdaroğlu: Mavi Marmara'ya İzin Vermezdik," *Hürriyet*, March 03, 2011, http://www.hurriyet.com.tr/gundem/17172761.asp (accessed July 11, 2011).

significant. In past parliamentary debates, it was usually opposition parties and the CHP that made anti-Israeli declarations and criticized the AKP for not taking a stronger stance against Tel Aviv. Twice, in 2005 and 2006, the CHP defeated an AKP proposal that state enterprises be sold to Israeli investors.[23]

Perhaps ironically, secularists and conservatives alike accuse the AKP of serving Zionist and Jewish interests. Shortly before the 2007 elections, the late leader of the National Outlook movement, Necmettin Erbakan, claimed that the Justice and Development Party was the "subcontractor" of Zionism and that Israel was attempting to bring the AKP to power once again.[24] Similarly, secularist political parties in Turkey have accused the AKP of cooperating with Israel and the United States in their effort to create moderately Islamic regimes in the Middle East and control the region. A series of books published in 2007, with such titles as *The Children of Moses*, *The Rose of Moses*, and *The Warrior of Moses,* argued that the leadership of the AKP was in close cooperation with Zionism. The books became bestsellers and were hailed by well-known secularist intellectuals. The underlying motivation in such allegations was to damage the standing of the party as the representative of pious Muslims and thereby weaken its electoral base. Apart from whether or not this strategy has worked, it is clear that accusations of Zionism have forced the AKP to prove its position even more passionately. The end result has been the escalation of anti-Israeli discourse in politics.

Public opinion surveys carried out since the 1990s show that conservatism in Turkey is on the rise. A study based on the findings of a survey conducted in 2006 demonstrates that the main components of this conservatism include religiosity, xenophobia, and intolerance. Close to 70 percent of the respondents placed themselves at the religious end of a scale running from 0 to 10 (10 being very religious). Around 75 percent of those who participated in the survey scored more than 50 points out of a 0 to 100 scale measuring xenophobia. Similarly, 68 percent obtained a score higher than 50 on a political

---

23. Gökhan Bacık, "Turkish-Israeli Relations after Davos: A View From Turkey," *Insight Turkey,* Vol. 11, No. 2 (2009), pp. 31-37.

24. "Erbakan, AK Parti ve CHP'ye Trabzon'dan yüklendi," *Zaman,* July 06, 2007, http://www.zaman.com.tr/haber.do?haberno=560876&keyfield=657262616B616E (accessed March 12, 2011), also in Bacık, "Turkish-Israeli Relations after Davos," p. 36.

intolerance scale.[25] These results indicate that Turkish conservatism brings together religious and nationalist elements. Thus, most of the Middle Eastern policies of the AKP that are attributed to its Islamist stance should be reinterpreted as attempts to capture these nationalist voters. As Ziya Öniş rightly notes, "The assertive and independent style of foreign policy making has had an appeal to nationalistic sentiments going well beyond the religious conservative core which had previously constituted the backbone of the AKP's support."[26] This strategy of appealing to both conservative and nationalist voters seems to have worked in the June 12, 2011 elections. While the AKP increased its share of votes by more than three percent from the 2007 elections and received 50 percent of the electorate's approval, the nationalist MHP's share of the ballot decreased 1.28 percent and the party received 13 percent of the votes.

Conservatism in Turkey is closely related to the electorate's perceptions of Europe, the United States, and Israel. Since 2005, the number of people that support Turkish membership in the European Union has been decreasing, and in 2007, one-third of the respondents of an election survey regarded the European Union as a threat more serious than Iran. Similar results were obtained with regards to anti-Americanism. In the summer of 2007, 80 percent of the respondents regarded the United States as more or less threatening, and more than half perceived the United States as a very serious threat. The attitudes of the participants toward Israel followed the United States as the second most threatening country, with more than 40 percent of the population regarding Israel as dangerous. It is noteworthy that such perceptions seem to be the same among the AKP, CHP and nationalist MHP voters.[27] Since the war in Iraq, significant numbers of people in Turkey believe that the United States is on a crusade against Muslims and supports Kurdish separatism, the most important domestic threat that Turkey faces. As Ömer Taşpınar nicely sums up the situation: "When you have a domestic public opinion that is resentful of American foreign policy and a prime

---

25. Ali Çarkoğlu and Ersin Kalaycıoğlu, *The Rising Tide of Conservatism in Turkey* (New York: Palgrave Macmillan, 2009), p. 27-63.
26. Ziya Öniş, "Multiple Faces of the 'New' Turkish Foreign Policy Underlying Dynamics and a Critique," *Insight Turkey*, Vol. 13, No. 1 (2011), p. 57.
27. Çarkoğlu and Kalaycıoğlu, *The Rising Tide*, pp. 121-139.

minister who really cares about what the 'Turkish street' thinks, there emerges a combustible mix."[28]

It is not only the AKP government and opposition parties that use nationalism to increase their share of votes. The media also capitalizes on such sentiments and further inflames people's feelings toward Israel. In 2009, for example, an episode of a TV series showed Israelis killing a Palestinian baby and raping Palestinian women in prison.[29] A year later, another TV series, which has broken viewer records, depicted Israeli soldiers attacking Turkish babies and killing innocent civilians. An earlier spinoff of the show, the movie entitled "Valley of Wolves: Iraq," portrayed American soldiers in similar pejorative terms.[30]

The dangerous mix of populist political parties, sensationalist media, and a nationalist public opinion has occasionally led to alarming protests in the streets. Between 2008 and 2010, on several occasions, crowds that were outraged by the events in Gaza or a new crisis between Israel and Turkey gathered in the streets of Istanbul, Ankara, and other cities. Protestors verbally threatened the Jewish minority in Turkey, shouted anti-Semitic slogans, and burned Israeli flags. Civil society organizations are sometimes responsible for these gatherings of thousands of people. Although some of these interest groups do not have any particular affiliation with a political party, one foundation, which is associated with the National Outlook movement, was reported to be behind some of these protests.[31]

It was another Islamic non-governmental organization, the Foundation for Human Rights and Freedoms and Humanitarian Relief (IHH), that coordinated the aid flotilla to Gaza that in May 2010 sparked a new crisis between Israel and Turkey. This type of civil society activism in foreign policy is relatively new. In the 1990s, Turkish foreign policy decision-making was monopolized by the Ministry of Foreign Affairs and the military. This was when Israel and Turkey

28. Ömer Taşpınar, "The Rise of Turkish Gaullism: Getting Turkish-American Relations Right," *Insight Turkey,* Vol. 13, No. 1 (2011), p. 15.
29. "'Ayrılık' Filistinliler'i de Kızdırdı," *HaberTurk,* April 05, 2010, http://www.haberturk.com/medya/haber/505790-ayrilik-filistinlileri-de-kizdirdi (accessed March 13, 2011).
30. "'A TV Series Is Not Only A TV Series' Diplomatic Crisis Show," *Today's Zaman,* January 17, 2010, http://todayszaman.com/newsDetail_getNewsById.action;jsessionid=9A6099B09AA16E24C97BE97CE46C4F8C?newsId=198780 (accessed March 13, 2011).
31. Aytürk , "Between Crises and Cooperation," p. 61.

started to cooperate in strategic and military matters. However, since the early 2000s, the state bureaucracy and the military lost some of their influence in foreign policy decisions. This was partially due to the democratization reforms that the AKP carried out in its first term in office, which decreased the veto and tutelary powers of the military in Turkish domestic politics. As a consequence, the government and (with its encouragement) civil society groups became more influential in foreign policy decision-making.

In a country where public opinion is conservative, nationalist, and anti-Western, civil society groups can be expected to share similar leanings. Turkey's alliance with Israel has never been based on non-military and non-bureaucratic interests. Thus, while Turkish civil society groups, especially businessmen, are eager to cooperate with neighboring economies, they do not actively pursue similar relations with Israel. The fact that there are no influential groups in foreign policy decision-making that advocate for cooperation with Israel partially explains the deteriorating relations between the two countries. Moreover, since the state elite cannot "control" foreign policy as much as they used to, "U.S.-Turkish relations are [now] more difficult to manage," as Larrabee has noted.[32]

## Conclusion

Since 2002, the AKP government has embarked on a leadership role in the Middle East. One direct consequence of this foreign policy objective has been the changes incurred in the American-Israeli-Turkish alliance. The AKP's so-far unsuccessful goal of mediating the Arab-Israeli conflict and its use of populist discourse to appeal to Middle Eastern populations set Ankara at odds with Washington and Tel Aviv. Despite the increasing anti-Israeli and anti-Western rhetoric of the AKP leadership, the essentials of Turkish foreign policy since the late 1990s have remained the same. In the aftermath of the Cold War, the strategic priorities and calculations of Ankara had to change. In the new international context, the coalition government that ruled Turkey before the AKP, started a foreign policy that was focused on having good relations with neighbors, using multilateral and diplomatic channels (instead of military might) to solve conflicts, and assuming a leadership role in the wider region. Thus, it is possible to trace some AKP policies to the earlier government.

32. Larrabee, "The 'New Turkey' and American-Turkish Relations," p. 4.

This is not to say that the Justice and Development Party did not have any contributions to shaping the new Turkish foreign policy. On the contrary, the AKP has successfully brought these strategies together, pursued them consistently and blended foreign policy objectives with a populist discourse. The AKP has also carried out important democratic reforms at home, which decreased the role of the military and bureaucracy in shaping foreign policy decisions. Yet, it is important to remember that none of these policies have necessarily been related to the AKP's Islamic roots. Since 2002, the party has adopted a cautious, ambiguous, and inconsistent policy toward one of the most important issues in Turkey's religious political movement—the issue of cooperating with Israel. Instead of completely abandoning all diplomatic contact, the AKP has striven to keep the channels of dialogue open and has not discontinued military cooperation. The fact that the previous secularist government pursued similar policies is strong evidence that if Turkey was ruled by a different political party, its basic foreign policy toward Israel and the United States would have been about the same.

The current stance of opposition political parties on the Israeli-Palestinian conflict and U.S.-Turkish relations is further evidence that the main elements of Turkish foreign policy transcend party politics and ideological convictions. Survey data shows that the majority of the Turkish electorate is conservative, religious, xenophobic, nationalist, anti-American, and anti-Israeli. In such a domestic context, political parties cannot afford to alienate these groups by publicly advocating a closer alliance with the United States and Israel. Now that civil society organizations and the media have more influence over Turkish citizens and foreign policy, it is not possible to conclude this paper with an optimistic prediction. It does not look likely that the new AKP government that was formed after the June 2011 elections will alter Turkey's relations with the United States and Israel significantly.

8

# Israel and Turkey: Domestic Politics and Foreign Policy

*Daniel Levy, New America Foundation*

## Overview

This paper will suggest that most of the reshaping of the Israeli-Turkish relationship has been driven by changes over the past decade on the Israeli side. In particular, during the Lieberman/ Netanyahu government there has been a confluence of domestic political considerations (driven by Foreign Minister Avigdor Lieberman) and of Israel's ideological positioning that has caused a significant deterioration in bilateral relations. This has been best summed up by Shlomo Brom, in a piece in *Haaretz*:

> Another recent example of this pervasive tendency is the way we deal with the Israeli-Turkish relationship. We perceive Israel's foreign relations as having only two shades: black and white. Either a state is friendly toward Israel and willing to accept anything we do, including our mischief, or it is an enemy—anti-Semitic and a member of the 'axis of evil'. Rarely do we assume that the explanation may be a bit more complicated, or search for the real reason for a foreign government's behavior.[1]

This short paper will argue that the good news is that Israeli public opinion is being led rather than leading in this reshaping of relations. The

1. Shlomo Brom, "Making an enemy of Ankara," *Haaretz*, November 12, 2009.

bad news is that the Israeli-Turkish fallout is increasingly also being played out in Washington, and that trend, being promoted by Israel's overzealous friends, may be more difficult to reverse.

What has been the role of Justice and Development Party (AKP)-led Turkey in the deterioration of relations?

The worldview of the AKP leadership would, in itself have posed new challenges to a more intense and mutually supportive set of Israeli-Turkish relations, which witnessed their heyday under a less democratic and Kemalist/military-led Turkey. Several factors encouraged Turkey to balance its previous Western orientation with a turn eastward to the region and beyond: the AKP's moderate Islamist orientation, the freezing of Turkey's accession talks to the European Union, the United States's loss of credibility in the region during the George W. Bush years, and the overall recalibration of the map of global and political economic power. This policy shift by Turkey has certainly happened, as can be seen in the way in which AKP-led Turkey has framed its foreign policy (the "zero problems" approach and a greater involvement in its neighborhood) and in its economic orientation, with a series of initiatives which have removed trade and visa restrictions between Turkey and its Arab backyard (notably with Syria, Jordan, Iraq, and Lebanon).

Two factors might have exacerbated this trend when it comes to the particulars of how Turkey has related to Israel in recent years. One has been an escalation of Israeli policies that are deeply unpopular in the Muslim world. This has made the AKP's and in particular Prime

---

*. . . most of the reshaping of the Israel/Turkey relationship has been driven by changes over the past decade on the Israeli side.*

---

Minister Recep Tayyip Erdoğan's positions vis-à-vis Israel popular at home and beyond, and therefore politically self-serving. The other is the personalities involved, notably Prime Minister Erdoğan and Foreign Minister Ahmet Davutoğlu, both of whom, and in particular the former, place a premium on being treated with respect in their conduct of international relations—respect being a behavioral trait which appears to not come easily to some within Israel's current leadership.

It would, however, be mistaken to attribute excessive causality to the AKP leadership in this story, for the following reasons:

- Impatience and frustrations with Israeli policy do not exclusively reside with the AKP or its constituents; they are in fact widespread across Turkey's political parties and its electorate. It is not unreasonable to suggest that given Israeli policy over the last decade, Turkey's approach would not have been too different no matter who was in power. In fact, the AKP has been criticized on occasion by the more secular and nationalist opposition parties for being too soft on Israel. Foreign Minister Davutoğlu was, for instance, criticized in Parliament following a meeting he held with then Israeli Minister Binyamin Ben-Eliezer after the flotilla incident.
- Turkey, under the AKP, has shown a clear capacity for pragmatism in its relations with Israel. There are a number of examples of this, including the state visit to Turkey by President Shimon Peres in November 2007; Turkey's not making an issue of Israeli over-flight of Turkish airspace during the apparent Israeli bombing raid of a suspected Syrian nuclear facility in the Deir ez-Zor region in 2007; Turkish agreement to Israeli accession to the OECD (all existing OECD member states, including Turkey, having the right of veto); and attempts to find common ground following first Operation Cast Lead (with Israeli Foreign Minister Tzipi Livni meeting Turkey's Foreign Minister Ali Babacan in March of 2009), and then the flotilla incident (the aforementioned Davutoğlu/Ben-Eliezer meeting).

## The 'Golden Era' of Israel's Relations with AKP-led Turkey

During the tenure of Prime Minister Ehud Olmert, Israel engaged in constructive working relations with AKP-led Turkey—and this, during a period that did not want for tension-raising developments. During Olmert's tenure (April 2006-March 2009) Israel undertook a major military operation in Lebanon in July/August 2006 and Operation Cast Lead in Gaza in December 2008, upgraded its closure policy against Gaza, and reportedly traversed Turkish airspace to attack Syria. Turkey hosted the Hamas leadership, maintained ongoing channels to Hamas, and openly and outspokenly criticized Israeli policies during this same period. Nevertheless, it was a time characterized by close, productive, and by all accounts mutually trusting relations between the Israeli and Turkish leaders.

Most notably, of course, this was the period during which Turkey, and in particular Prime Minister Erdoğan and his senior advisor Davutoğlu, acted as mediators in negotiations between Israel and Syria (intriguingly in this instance, Israel and Turkey were teaming up to pursue an approach that was frowned upon by the Bush administration).

There was an ongoing intensity of Israeli-Turkish exchanges, including frequent meetings and phone calls between the respective leaders; and the role of trusted mediator conferred by Israel on Prime Minister Erdoğan was one that had traditionally been the preserve of very few third parties and certainly very few non-Americans. It was also a period when Israeli-Turkish trade and military ties continued to flourish. One conclusion is undoubtedly that the personalities matter—at its most basic level, Erdoğan and Olmert felt they could get on and do business with each other. Beyond that, this period demonstrated ability on both sides to disagree where necessary and cooperate where it made sense. Although that is hardly something original in international relations or in the way that Turkey manages its global affairs, it is the precise antithesis to the Brom description, quoted above, of the current Israeli predisposition in its diplomatic relations, wherein you are with us or against us.

## Politics and Ideology Come Together with the Netanyahu/Lieberman Government

The politics is relatively simple to explain. Netanyahu formed a right-wing government, which of course draws its support from a right-wing constituency in Israel, including the ultra-religious and ultra-nationalist blocs. From an early stage in the Netanyahu government, it became clear that Lieberman, who serves as both foreign minister and the leader of the *Yisrael Beiteinu* party, had decided that his political strategy vis-à-vis Prime Minister Netanyahu and the Likud Party was to outflank them from the right.

Lieberman understood that, as prime minister, Netanyahu would have to at least speak in more temperate terms, an obligation that did not have to extend to all government ministers. Lieberman and his deputy minister, Danny Ayalon, therefore chose to use their perches at the foreign ministry in order to demonstrate an unprecedented bluntness in the conduct of Israel's international affairs. This was a way not only of playing to their existing base on the nationalistic right, but also of reaching out to Netanyahu/Likud supporters with the suggestion that the prime minister was going soft. Turkey—being led by an Islamist party, and having been critical of Israel over Cast Lead and following the Davos incident—was a perfect candidate for Lieberman's new style of "diplomacy."

*There is now a quite clear campaign to discredit AKP-led Turkey in the United States.*

In January 2010, Deputy Foreign Minister Ayalon publicly humiliated the Turkish ambassador to Israel and made sure that television cameras were there to record the event. The political team at the foreign ministry has taken a highly belligerent posture toward Turkey and has vociferously and publicly come out against any compromise over the flotilla incident that might entail an Israeli apology. In this respect, the Lieberman effect has been a pronounced one in determining the deteriorating trajectory of bilateral relations.

The politics and personality of the role played by Lieberman might be fleeting; however, the Netanyahu government's position vis-à-vis Turkey goes deeper into the realm of the ideology, political positioning, and the narrative of Israel's current right-wing government. It seems that the position that has been adopted toward Turkey might be called Israel's own version of "the Turkey model." It consists of the following: Israel does not want a precedent to be established whereby one can be enough of an ally of Israel to a) be a trusted mediator; b) have normal working bilateral relations; and c) avoid Israeli opprobrium on the international stage and in particular in the United States, and yet also be critical of Israeli policies in a way that is challenging to Israel on the international stage (in other words, not just paying lip service). Israel has in the past grown accustomed to not having to deal with relations of this nature. Egypt under Hosni Mubarak did not dare to challenge Israeli policies in the ways that Erdoğan did.

The precedent was especially unwelcome coming from a Muslim country that is part of the region. For an Israel that would maintain control of the Palestinians and resulting policies, there is a structural logic to taking the approach that Netanyahu has pursued and to attempting to draw starker lines in regard to who constitutes an ally. Israeli policy toward Turkey under Netanyahu therefore makes sense in the context of an Israeli narrative which views any criticism as delegitimization, which sets a low bar for belonging to a hostile axis, and which is *a priori* opposed to Islamists in the political arena.

At home, the government has rallied much of the media, its own constituency, and the public beyond that to a position that depicts Turkey as an enemy and part of the resistance axis with Iran, Hamas, and Syria. Israel has, of course, also tried to promote this line internationally. The Netanyahu government has even pursued a set of foreign relations with this in mind. If Israel used to think in terms of an alliance of the periphery (with Turkey, Iran, and Ethiopia), one might describe today's policy as one of seeking allies in the super-periphery, with a significant investment having been made in improving Israel's strategic ties with Greece, mostly it seems as an attempt to poke a finger in Turkey's eye. Greece's prime minister visited Israel, which was reciprocated by Netanyahu in August 2010. Israel has also been drawing closer to Cyprus. Meanwhile, Israel's friends in the Conference of Presidents of Major American Jewish Organizations paid their first leadership visit to Greece in February 2011, while also promoting legislation in Congress supported by the Greek lobby in America.

## What Is Easy to Repair and What Is Not

The current state of play would suggest that Israeli-Turkish relations have reached a level of hostility that would be difficult to reverse, given that the respective publics seem to be on board for this parting of ways. There were popular demonstrations against Israel in Turkey following the flotilla incident and *vice versa*. Nevertheless, on both sides, it would be wise not to get carried away. To the extent to which the publics are on board, this would seem to be more about each other's policies rather than a deep or more ethnically/racially–driven prejudice. Turkey was a major tourist destination for Israelis, and it is not difficult to envisage Israeli opinion swinging back with relative ease. In addition, there are voices among Israel's elites, whether in the security and diplomatic establishment or in the business community, who are deeply uncomfortable with this negative turn in bilateral relations. And even during the period of the Netanyahu government, there have been attempts to set relations more on an even keel. For instance, Netanyahu was due to meet with Davutoğlu in Washington just before the flotilla incident; Turkey sent fire-extinguishing and rescue assistance during the Carmel forest fire of December 2010; and there were attempts to find language to resolve the flotilla issue subsequent to that Turkish gesture. Such attempts will no doubt continue to be pursued, especially once the UN Secretary General–mandated inquiry into the flotilla incident produces its report. Diplomatic relations have, of course, not been suspended.

However, given the current personal composition and political/ideological positioning of the Netanyahu government, it is difficult to envisage any improvement in the short term. In fact, Israel shows every indication of continuing to hunker down and turn ever more in on itself. There are, of course, also ways in which Turkey and Israel's regional ambitions are not complementary.

Overall though, Turkey might be seen as a powerful example of the terrain on which a battle is being fought between what one might call "realists" and "denialists" in Israel. That has been made all the more stark by the recent changes in the region and what those might presage. Arab regimes in the Middle East that are more responsive to public opinion might well pursue policies toward Israel that more closely resemble those of Turkey under the AKP.

Israeli realists will suggest that Israel will have to adjust to this reality by, among other things, changing its approach to the Palestinians and being less absolutist in its demands of those with whom it has relations. The denialists will have Israel attempt to ally itself ever more closely with the West—as they try to convince Western publics that they are in a common civilizational struggle with Israel against radical Islam—and would "dig in," in policy terms. That the denialists are currently very much in the ascendency is borne out in Israel's policy toward Turkey.

## Israel versus Turkey in the United States

One arena in which this deteriorating relationship has most resonance and where some of the more worrying fallout is occurring is in the United States. For many years, Israel's supporters in Washington helped to mobilize in support of Turkey, notably around preventing resolutions on the Armenian Genocide issue. But in June 2010, Eli Lake reported in *The Washington Times* that:

> [T]he American Jewish community is no longer helping Turkey, after a tumultuous deterioration of ties between Israel and Turkey in the past four years . . . . In some ways, the Memorial Day flotilla affair marks an end of

Israel's more than 20-year strategic alliance with Turkey, and the resulting support from the pro-Israel lobby in Washington.[2]

There is now a quite clear campaign to discredit AKP-led Turkey in the United States, including in Congress. This campaign is being enthusiastically embraced, if not led, by forces that are very identified with Israel and with the establishment, pro-Israel movements.

Statements by staunchly pro-Israel members of Congress have taken a harshly anti-Turkey flavor of late. Leading lights among the traditional pro-Israel columnists and policy wonk community have taken to attacking Turkey, including Elliott Abrams,[3] Charles Krauthammer,[4] and Jackson Diehl.[5] The more truculent promoters of this tone have gone as far as labeling the AKP "Islamofascist"[6] (Frank Gaffney), while Daniel Pipes told Canadian Television, "Turkey is the long-term greatest threat to the West in the Middle East . . . . Turkey is no longer the bridge, it is now the problem."[7]

This could become even stickier than the direct problems generated by the fallout between the Israelis and Turks themselves. Turkey is well aware of these hostile initiatives in the United States and will undoubtedly not look kindly upon them. The dilemmas in the U.S.-Israeli relationship, which are real, albeit often skated over for political reasons, are likely to come into sharper relief given the strategic position that Turkey occupies in a mapping of contemporary American national security interests.

---

2. Eli Lake, "American Jewish community ends support of Turkish interests on Hill," *The Washington Times,* June 8, 2010.
3. Elliot Abrams, "A Turkey of a Policy," *The Weekly Standard,* June 21, 2010.
4. Charles Krauthammer, "The Fruits of Weakness," *National Review Online,* May 21, 2010.
5. Jackson Diehl, "How Wikileaks cables capture 21st-century Turkey," *Washington Post,* December 5, 2010.
6. Frank J. Gaffney Jr., "Islamofascism's Creeping Coup in Turkey," *Frontpagemag.com,* March 15, 2006.
7. Daniel Pipes, "Daniel Pipes is Off Iran: The Real Bad Guy is Turkey," *Political Correction,* December 16, 2010.

9

# Domestic Influences: Comments and Discussion

## *Allen Lynch:*

The first conclusion that I draw from the excellent papers that have been presented on this panel is that domestic politics definitely matters in the complex diplomatic relations among Turkey, Israel, and the United States, but that it matters in context. That context includes fluid internal political alignments in all three states as well as changing external conditions, e.g., the end of the Cold War, the impact of the terror attacks of September 11, 2001, and the revolts throughout the Arab world this past winter and spring. Indeed, these changing external factors themselves affect core political alignments at home, a fact that makes generalization and theorizing about the Turkish-U.S.-Israeli relationship exceedingly complex. And although it is true, as Philip Zelikow earlier observed, that much of everyday diplomacy is both inductive and reactive in character, it does not thereby follow that there are no patterns of significance to discern. Otherwise, events would literally be meaningless and there would be no point to this conference.

It is, for instance, a truism that political leaders, especially in democracies like the United States, Israel, and Turkey, hew to the broad contours of public opinion (or at least to what those contours will allow, or even more precisely, not unduly punish). Foreign policy thus inevitably tends to reflect domestic politics, to a degree. Few can doubt, whatever their policy preferences, that American policy toward the Israeli-Palestinian conflict is importantly, and at times decisively shaped, by the influence of the pro-Israeli lobby in American electoral and bureaucratic politics. It is a major irony that the range of politically acceptable debate on the Israeli-Palestinian dispute has usually been broader and more interesting in Tel Aviv than in Washington, D.C. Likewise, it is obvious that Israel's own diplomatic flexibility has been shaped, and over time constrained by, the major shift to the right that has taken place in Israeli politics since the mid-1990s. In this setting, fragile coalition governments that are politically hostage to extremist splinter factions dare not take risks for peace that would likely see their immediate ouster from power. And finally, Turkey's foreign policy orientation has undeniably been affected by the progressive democratization of the Turkish polity that elected the AKP government in 2002 that has been in power in Ankara ever since. As the secularist military has lost its grip on national politics, to be replaced by a government more representative of the country's overwhelming Muslim majority, the premises of alignment with Israel have become ever harder to defend in Turkish politics.

Yet domestic political alignments themselves are often affected by external circumstances. For instance, I would argue, contrary to much of the literature on the "democratic peace," that it is less democracy that produces international peace than it is international peace that is, in the long run, the most favorable framework condition for the emergence and consolidation of democracy. A liberalism that is, in effect, "in love with itself"—determined to reproduce itself wherever it can—can be quite bellicose. Think only of the United States freed of the external constraints of the Cold War: Columbia University's Richard Betts has made the point that the United States has been much more aggressively interventionist after, rather than during, the Cold War. Indeed, the United States has not used its military forces abroad so freely since the heyday of the Roosevelt Corollary to the Monroe Doctrine in the first decades of the twentieth century. So even mature liberal democracies are not per se pacifist, especially in a world populated by many illiberal regimes.

Moreover, high levels of external threat, or perceptions of threat, tend to correlate with governments that are more centralized rather than less, more authoritarian rather than less, more militarized rather than less, and more aggressive rather than less. The case could thus be made, "*Si vis democratiam, para pacem*—if you want democracy, prepare for peace."

Paradoxically, peace at the level of the international system, i.e., the end of the Cold War, has made peace in the Middle East harder to attain. The end of the Soviet "threat" has meant a much-reduced strategic incentive for American leaders to risk precious political capital on the Israeli-Palestinian conflict, while the complicating shift to the right in Israeli politics was propelled and reinforced by massive emigration from Russia since 1990, itself a byproduct of the end of the Cold War.

---

*. . . contrary to much of the literature on the "democratic peace," it is less democracy that produces international peace than it is international peace that is the most favorable condition for the emergence and consolidation of democracy.*

---

Other important examples of how international factors impact domestic political motives on regional diplomacy include: (a) the obvious hostility in France and Germany to Turkey's entry into the European Union and the effect that this had had on Turkey's European vocation (as when Nicholas Sarkozy called for a national referendum on any future Turkish entry into the European Union or when German Chancellor Angela Merkel stated flatly that the assimilationist project in Germany has "definitively failed"); (b) the negative effect that stalemate (at best) in Israeli-Palestinian relations has had on Turkey's willingness to give Israel the benefit of the doubt in a domestic climate where, as Yaprak Gürsoy argued in her paper, the majority is religious, xenophobic, intolerant, and anti-Zionist if not anti-Semitic, and the Turkish rapprochement with Israel, according to Henri Barkey, "always lacked domestic support;" and (c) the corresponding impact of the decline in Turkish-Israeli relations in lowering the barriers to U.S. domestic initiatives hostile to Turkey, such as the periodic Congressional attempt to hold the Turkish Republic to account for the Armenian Genocide committed under the Ottoman Empire.

Insofar as diplomatic choices are also political choices, then, external and internal factors interact in ways that tend to defy clear theorizing. Although democracy may have a positive effect on the prospects for peace, the possibility and durability of peace also affects the chances for the development and consolidation of democracy. External structural and internal political factors thus need to be examined in their complex interrelationships.

Moreover, and to complicate things further, "democracy," in the form of enduring, mature, and stable liberal- or social-democracies, is not the same thing as "democratization," or the creation of democracy from crumbled authoritarian, totalitarian, or simply despotic foundations. The long, often tumultuous and violent history of the emergence of democracy in the Western world demonstrates that there is an organic interdependence among a set of institutions that acts as the necessary framework for the consolidation of liberal democracy. These include a substantial market economy, to eliminate the chance that the state can dominate society through ownership of most land, labor, and capital; a functioning legal system, so that the holder of capital can calculate his or her odds of return and thus make the market economy function; as well as a reasonably capable and non-corrupt system of public administration, so that legal requirements can be identified and laws formulated, passed, and subsequently enforced. Over a long enough period of time, such conditions can allow for a society to emerge that is sufficiently prosperous and independent of public authority to be able to hold government to account. Yet keep in mind that in the United States, often thought to be the exemplary case of democratic development, it took 75 years until the Civil War determined—by bullet, not ballot—whether the country would be a federal democracy, a confederal democracy, or two democracies: one slave and one liberal. It would take another century before full democratic rights were extended to those African-Americans whose rights were formally guaranteed after the Civil War. So an element of modesty is in order before pronouncing on any automaticity of democratic political development, not to mention the relationship between democratization and international peace.

Indeed, in the country that I know best, Russia, American attempts in the 1990s to graft the institutions of free-market democracy onto a country with almost none of the institutional or cultural preconditions for it helped induce the first mass-based wave of anti-Americanism in the country's history. Ironically, today's Russia would be much more reflexively anti-American without the pragmatic Vladimir Putin's authoritarian grip on power. Relatedly, Jack Snyder and Edward Mansfield have argued that rapid post-authoritarian democratization tends to create political incentives for ambitious politicians to mobilize political majorities on nationalist grounds, hardly a prescription for harmonious international relations. The case of contemporary Turkey illustrates one aspect of their thesis: The rise of the AKP to power definitely reflects the growing democratization of the Turkish political and social order. Since the Turkish *demos* is predominantly Muslim, it has become harder for leaders to make the case for balanced ties with Israel, especially as the Israeli-Palestinian relationship remains fraught with tension and occasional violence: Vivid images of suffering Palestinians, whatever the context, can easily inflame mass emotions. In this setting, the government, or important factions within the government, tolerate and even encourage anti-Israeli and even anti-Semitic programming on the airwaves and movie theaters. Such displays may be intolerant and illiberal, but they are not undemocratic.

Turkey, of course, represents the best case, and for many it is a model, of democratic development in the Middle East. Even so, as Greg Gause notes in his paper, the extension of the current Turkish model of democratic development throughout the region entails many more complications for the United States compared to the days when Israel and Turkey, and by extension the United States, had a sound set of interrelationships.

What can be said in this light about the prospects for democracy arising out of the Arab revolt of late 2010–early 2011? First, it is clear that none of the countries in the region, save possibly Morocco, possesses a robust set of the institutions and traditions that typically accompany liberal democracy: a vibrant capitalism, rule of law, a public-spirited administration and civil service, as well as a custom of peaceable and law-governed transfer of national power. So, stable democratic outcomes are unlikely in the short run. Much more likely is an effort to reassert nationalist traditions in foreign policy, which inevitably means that Turkey, Egypt, and Iran will be competing for influence in a region whose configuration of politics and power will be much less certain for Israel than it has been in recent decades. The ouster of Mubarak has seen to that.

Yet for the United States, unlike Israel, this is really an opportunity. The core American geopolitical interest in the region, as distinct from its ideological interest, is not to extend liberal democracy throughout a region that is ill-suited for it in the short run, but rather to prevent any local power from assuming a hegemony that could be hostile to America's economic and security interests in the region. The early returns from Tunisia, Egypt, Turkey, and Iran suggest that there will be ample opportunity for the United States to exercise the role of regional balancer in the years ahead, domestic political realities permitting.

Finally, it is clear that, whatever the logic of geopolitics, the United States is not going to abandon its ideological vocation as the champion of democracy. "*Novus ordo seclorum*" ("A new order for the ages," inscribed on the Great Seal of the United States) is as central to American national identity as is "*E pluribus unum.*" Yet arguably, the best way to promote the emergence of genuine democracy in the region is to establish a framework of peace that reduces the incentives for aggressive political mobilization on nationalist grounds and allows the time—a long period of time—necessary for governments to be held accountable to their people, instead of *vice versa*.

Henry Stimson was once asked what it took to produce peace. He replied that you had to staff the government with people who believed in the possibility of peace, work them to the bone until they dropped of exhaustion, and then replace them with another group who also believed in peace. But first, of course, you have to believe in the possibility of peace itself.

## *Jeffrey Legro:*

The central question is what might explain the deterioration in the relationship between Turkey and Israel. The most significant domestic political development in Turkey seems to have been the rise of xenophobic, nationalist, anti-Western, and anti-Semitic thought. But what has led to these sentiments has yet to be adequately explained. A flourishing democratic atmosphere in Turkey may indeed be part of the answer.

The end of the Cold War is also another plausible explanation, yet it fails to account for the flux in Turkish-Israeli relations for the last twenty years. Although a decline in the perceived power of the United States, which no longer has the capability to reconcile differences between uncomfortable allies, may be another causal factor, it is difficult to argue that there has been such a dramatic decrease in U.S. power as to cause such a shift. The rise in Turkish ambition is another suggested explanation, yet its origins remain murky. Does the increase in regional ambition encourage nationalist, xenophobic thought or *vice versa*?

The change in Turkish domestic opinion may also be affected by the behavior of other actors toward Turkey and its perceived main threats. In particular, how others have treated the Kurdish issue may have influenced Turkey's attitudes toward others, thus heightening nationalistic, xenophobic, conservative public opinion. The Iraq War could have led to Iran and Syria being more supportive of Turkey, making the West seem less so. Moreover, the stalling in Turkey's EU accession talks perhaps also influenced the rise of nationalism and xenophobia in Turkish domestic opinion.

Yet the main cause of the rise of xenophobia and nationalism is often pinned on Israel's domestic policies: the Second Intifada, the decline of the Oslo peace process, Gaza closure policies, and the *Mavi Marmara* incident. If Israeli actions had been different, then Turkish public opinion would not be what it is today. Indeed, Israel's policies disappoint Turkish expectations that its relationship with Israel would alter Israel's actions. Israel's rightward shift only then delegitimizes Turkey's relations with Israel. This argument supports Barkey's assertion that Turkish-Israeli relations were built on fragile ground and are unsustainable in the long-term.

*The decline in Turkish-Israeli relations stems from rigid Israeli diplomacy, which then affects Turkish public opinion, resulting in a self-defeating game of tit for tat.*

In fact, the inflexibility of Israeli diplomacy in a post–Cold War era that is marked by dynamism may also be at the root of the decline in Israeli-Turkish relations. Whereas Turkey has a fluid diplomacy that adapts to regional changes, Israel's foreign policy remains ossified. The decline in Turkish-Israeli relations could be described as stemming from rigid Israeli diplomacy, which then affects Turkish public opinion. The mutually reinforcing relationship results in a self-defeating game of tit for tat whereby Turkey's regional ambitions depend on a diminishing Israeli role, which Israel will never allow. In analyzing Turkish-Israeli relations, the conceptual challenge remains how to understand the relationship between diplomacy and external politics in the region, and the nature of domestic politics, which will be taking shape in the days ahead.

## Discussion:

**Henri Barkey:** The single greatest factor behind this rising xenophobic sentiment in Turkey is the Kurdish question. This issue goes to the very nature of the Turkish state, which does not recognize that there is a minority that does not accept the dominant conception of the Turkish state. This causes incredible tension, undermining the notion that there is a single ethnic identity and one set of borders in Turkey, and that these are unchangeable. Meanwhile, the AKP continues to believe that the United States went to war in Iraq to create a Kurdish state and divide Turkey. Although Turkey has grandiose ambitions in the region, it also feels extraordinarily vulnerable. In fact, its goals are designed to mask its internal weaknesses. The biggest challenge for Turkey is how it will deal with the Kurdish question as it reemerges as a civil movement similar to Tunisia and Egypt. In short, xenophobia is a result of a Turkish identity crisis driven by the Kurdish question.

*What has changed is that democratization and the decreasing role of the military in politics now allow public opinion to be influential in shaping Turkish-American and Turkish-Israeli relations.*

**Yaprak Gürsoy:** Xenophobia is in fact merely Turkish conservatism. Moreover, it is not new. Rather, the Turkish public has always been nationalist and xenophobic. What has changed is that democratization and the decreasing role of the military in politics now allow public opinion to be influential in shaping Turkish-American and Turkish-Israeli relations. For instance, when the military was still the dominant actor in Turkish politics, there was only one state-controlled television channel. Given that several news channels exist today, public opinion has a bigger arena to shape politics. Although the degree to which public opinion can affect Turkish foreign policy is exaggerated, the fact that it has the ability to influence policy at all is a new phenomenon in Turkey.

**Daniel Levy:** We may now see more of this in the Middle East. In the case of Turkey, the key variable is whether its more democratic nature makes it responsive to public opinion. If post–Arab Spring governments adopt the Turkish model, the power of public opinion to influence policy will be put to the test, which is an outcome that the Israelis dread. Hosni Mubarak was very user-friendly to the Israelis; however, the Israeli government will no longer have such regional support if Arab governments become more receptive to public opinion.

Indeed, xenophobic, nationalist public opinion in Israel was clearly manifested during the Egyptian Revolution. By reading the Israeli press during the demonstrations, one would have thought that Obama had sent the protesters to Tahrir Square! Right-wing Israeli public attitudes pose a problem for recalibrating Turkish-Israeli relations. This is only further complicated by an overzealous pro-Israel community in the U.S. that is eager to follow orders and create problems for Turkey. It is clear that the first leadership mission to Greece of the major American Jewish organizations was meant to send a signal to Turkey. In fact, the goal was to influence Turkish domestic politics by making it appear that the AKP was damaging the Turkish-American relationship.

**Soli Özel:** The issue of rampant xenophobia is in fact a political problem. If it is viewed as a public opinion problem, we avoid the political issue that is at its center, which is a lack of peace stemming primarily from the Palestinian issue. Given the paralysis of Israeli domestic politics and complicating factors such as the likely UN recognition of an independent Palestinian state, can the Palestinian question ever be resolved? If the situation remains deadlocked, then the most important political issue in the region will worsen, becoming further complicated by mobilized domestic groups.

**Questioner:** Xenophobia is an inaccurate description of Turkish public opinion. While there has been a rise in anti-Western and anti-Israeli discourse and attitudes, there has not been a dramatic increase in xenophobia. In fact, the lack of an ethno-nationalist government in power has

*The post-Oslo environment had created conducive conditions for Israelis, Palestinians, Turks and Arabs to meet and discuss common interests.*

made Turkey more capable of engaging with ethnic groups such as the Armenians and Kurds. Indeed, anti-Westernism is a reaction to regional policy. If policy decisions had been handled differently, particularly by the United States, how would the situation contrast with that of today? The post-Oslo environment had created conducive conditions for Israelis,

Palestinians, Turks, and Arabs to meet and discuss common interests. It is difficult to imagine that the United States' mishandling of the Israeli-Palestinian issue has not led to the current lack of tangible progress.

**Yaprak Gürsoy:** I agree with the questioners. Policies toward the United States and Israel were similar before the AKP came to power and thus cannot be attributed merely to public opinion or the rise of conservatism. Rather, strategic relations and international politics are also important.

**Daniel Levy:** It is very difficult to know what the Israeli government wants. Theoretically the United States could play a role in resolving the Palestinian issue, but domestic Israeli politics will not allow for that to happen. As to the second question, it is very difficult to side with Arab freedom, but not the Palestinian problem, shedding light on American hypocrisy concerning the issue.

**Henri Barkey:** American hypocrisy indeed exists, but hypocrisy is a global problem. It is true that had the Palestinian issue been solved, it would have alleviated a number of problems. But for Turkey, the majority of difficulties with Washington have more to do with Iran and not the Israeli-Palestinian issue.

**Allen Lynch:** If we accept that Arab-Israeli peace is the key regional issue, then American policy is the key external variable in achieving it. Then the question becomes, do we have a government that believes in the possibility of peace?

Part IV

# The Iranian Factor

*When the conference was being planned in fall 2010, Iran seemed to be the substantive issue area where the divergences in policy among the United States, Turkey, and Israel could be most clearly seen. After all, Turkey had been arguing strenuously for a policy of engagement, Israel was calling for more assertive policies, including the possibility of military attacks, and the United States was caught somewhere in between, dabbling with engagement while hoping that deterrence and sanctions could bring about deep-seated change in Tehran.*

*By the time the conference was held, the Middle East was experiencing the full flowering of the "Arab Spring." Iran was still an issue for our primary three countries, but so also was the new order that might emerge in the Arab world. Egypt was possibly showing a more self-confident and independent streak in its dealings with the region. Syria was in turmoil, which could affect its immediate neighbors as well as political movements that had counted on support from Damascus. And of course, Iran itself would be affected if Egypt gained more influence within the region and if Syria changed from its long-standing pro-Iran stance.*

*To assess these developments from the perspective of Iran, I invited Trita Parsi, the author of a remarkable book on another key "triangular" relationship in the region, that among the United States, Israel, and Iran. Iranian by origin, educated at Yale, and fully a part of the Washington policy scene, Parsi brought to our gathering a fresh and lively appreciation of Iran's quest for regional influence and of its attempt to gain soft power that would enhance its influence in a region in which its Persian and Shiite identities left it with few natural allies. Playing the pro-Palestinian, anti-Israel card has been one way Iran's rulers have hoped to achieve this.*

*Responding to Parsi were two Iranian-Americans with long ties to the University of Virginia, Ruhi Ramazani and Farzaneh Milani. The former launched the study of the modern Middle East at the university in the 1950s, and the latter is now the chair of the Department of Middle East and South Asian Languages and Cultures. Both have written extensively on Iran, Ramazani on Iranian foreign policy in particular, and Milani on Iran's culture and literature.*

*Drawing on his sense of history, Ramazani sketched a picture of a Middle East in which the "big three" regional powers—Turkey, Egypt, and Iran—would be vying for regional influence. Each could draw on certain assets, but none could hope to dominate the entire region. Milani, arguing that literature could provide insights into the thoughts of ordinary citizens, concluded that the striving for democracy by peoples of the region could not be turned back. A new Middle East would, she felt sure, emerge.*

*~WBQ*

10

# Iran, Israel, the United States, and Turkey in a Changing Middle East Environment

*Trita Parsi, National Iranian American Council*

The Middle East is experiencing a political earthquake with few parallels in recent memory. With the overthrow of Hosni Mubarak in Egypt and Zine El-Abidine Ben Ali in Tunisia, and the ongoing struggles in Yemen, Libya, and Bahrain, all the states in the region—or involved in the region—have had to reassess their positions, alliances, and policies. These developments have also once and for all shattered the frames through which the Middle East was understood, or presented, by various governments. The defining struggle is not between "moderates" and "radicals," at least not if the definition of moderate is an Arab state that is an ally of the United States and at virtual peace with Israel.[1] The dictatorships that have fallen thus far all fell in the category of the old definition of moderates. Similarly, the struggle is not between Islamic and secular forces. The rallying call of the protesters in Tunisia and Egypt was democracy and dignity, not Islam and Sharia.[2] The extent to

1. Robert Malley and Peter Harling, "Shifting Allegiances in Middle East Mean Opportunities for President Obama," *Washington Post,* March 6, 2010, p. A15.
2. R.K. Ramazani, "Democracy, Not Islam, Is the Solution?" *The Daily Progress,* March 7, 2011, accessed June 27, 2011.

which the protests in Bahrain have taken on a sectarian tone is arguably due to the efforts of the ruling Bahraini regime and its allies in Saudi Arabia—both considered "moderates" in the old frame—and not because of the protesters.

These developments have shocked a region already besieged by an intense rivalry between Israel and the United States on the one hand, and Iran on the other. The shock has not ended this rivalry, but it has changed the context and created both challenges and opportunities for all sides. Israel faces a severe strategic challenge. In the past three decades, it has lost some of its most important regional allies and partners. Over the course of a decade after the 1979 Iranian Revolution, Israel's most important periphery ally, Iran, turned from friend to foe. In the past few years, the second most important periphery ally, Turkey, has also seen its interests diverge from those of Tel Aviv. Turkish-Israeli ties have hit an all-time low and, in the view of many analysts, the old Israeli-Turkish alliance cannot be resurrected. Then, on February 11, 2011, Israel lost its most important Arab partner: the Mubarak government in Egypt. The Mubarak regime's strong collaboration with Israel against Hamas and Iran was revealed when WikiLeaks released U.S. diplomatic cables discussing these affairs.

To make matters worse for Israel, the latest losses have coincided with an unusual period of tensions between Israel and the United States caused by their diverging interests. The United States has recognized that the status quo in the region is untenable and is struggling to define itself on the side of the democratization movement without damaging its other strategic interests in the region—including its support for Israel. Tel Aviv, on the other hand, views regional developments quite differently. Martin Kramer of Israel's conservative Shalem Center put his finger on the central point of contention between the United States and Israel during the Herzliya Conference in Israel in February 2011. Questioning the U.S. contention that the regional status quo is unsustainable, Kramer said the following: "In Israel, we are for the status quo. Not only do we believe the status quo is sustainable, we think it's the job of the U.S. to sustain it."[3]

For Iran, recent regional developments have strengthened its hands in the short run, but its ability to profit from the fall of pro-American dictatorships in the long run is uncertain. The decline of the United States

3. Matthew Duss, "Letter from Herzliya, Neocon Woodstock," *The Nation*, February 14, 2011.

in the region, which had been ongoing since the invasion of Iraq and is increasingly evident through the recent "people revolutions," has created a power and leadership vacuum that begs to be filled. Iran, and especially its hard-liners, has waited for the moment when the Arab street would rise up against the Arab regimes—though Iran thought this moment would include the Arab street also rising up against America. Despite the fact that Iran has long cherished this moment, at the end of the day it is not the only contender.

To understand Iranian behavior, one must first understand Iran's objectives and the cards it has been dealt. Iran is a majority Shiite, Persian state in a region dominated by Sunnis and/or Arabs. It has historically suffered from an acute sense of strategic loneliness in the region: Iran has no obvious partners or allies in the region, and its experience with extra-regional superpowers has left it convinced that it can rely only on itself for its security. Perhaps somewhat surprisingly, there are striking similarities between Israel and Iran in this regard. Yet, in spite of its strategic loneliness, distinctive ethnicity, and sectarian uniqueness, Iran's conventional superiority, resources, and rich culture have enabled it to play the role of a regional superpower over the millennia. By now, the notion that Iran is destined to be first among equals—*primus inter pares*—in the decision-making of the region is deeply ingrained in the Iranian identity—regardless of the nature of the regime governing Iran. Paradoxically, Iran is the odd man out in a region that it nevertheless seeks to lead.

Modern history has taught the Iranians that hard power alone will not enable them to achieve regional leadership. Although Tehran's Arab neighbors recognized Iran's military superiority in the 1970s, the late Shah of Iran aptly understood that he could neither obtain nor maintain a position of preeminence in the Persian Gulf through arms and oil alone; Iran needed to be seen as a legitimate power in the eyes of the Arabs as well. The Shah realized that Iran could not always treat the Arabs as enemies and balance them through Iranian military preponderance. Not only was a more conciliatory policy necessary to gain legitimacy for Iran's domination, but Iran also had to befriend the Arabs to most efficiently guarantee its long-term security. By the mid-1970s, Iran was at its peak. It had befriended Egypt, neutralized Iraq, quadrupled its oil income, and established its unsurpassed position in the Middle East. Yet, the Shah

4. Trita Parsi, "Whither the Persian-Jewish alliance?" *bitterlemons-international.org*, December 16, 2004.

never managed to bridge the Sunni-Shiite or the Persian Arab divide. To achieve these aims, he needed soft power, which his Iran lacked.[4]

The Islamic revolutionaries who took power in 1979 recognized this same reality and sought to bridge the divide with the Arabs through the ideology of political Islam. Although this strategy was abysmally unsuccessful with the Arab regimes—the ruling Arab elites feared the ideological force of the Persian clerics more than the military force of the Shah—Iran's brand of political Islam and anti-imperialist posture has won it coveted soft power on the Arab street. In fact, Iran's claim to leadership in the region is not based on Iran's nonexistent military superiority, but rather on its material support for various political groups in the region and its ability to exploit the frustration of the Arab and Muslim masses over perceived injustices in the region, including both regional political issues such as the Israeli-Palestinian conflict and domestic political issues.

Recent regional developments have shown not only the relevance of the Arab street, but also its ability to play a decisive role for the region's future. In fact, if the democracy wave that swept Tunisia and Egypt continues to conquer the region, it will test both the powers that invested in the order that suppressed the Arab street as well as the powers that claimed to champion it. This is likely the new fault line in the region, one that will intensify the rivalry between the United States and Iran for dominance in the region, and may also lead to a new rivalry between Turkey and Iran as Ankara increasingly positions itself to challenge Tehran's attempt to fill the vacuum left by a declining America. The questions facing Iran read as follows: If Iran's main instrument for achieving regional leadership has been its soft power, which in turn has been rooted in Iran's anti-American and anti-Israeli posture, in addition to material support to various political groups, then will the recent changes in the region enable Iran to exploit the victory of the Arab street? Or, will the emergence of a more confident and empowered Arab populace undermine the foundation of the Islamic Republic's soft power? Is Iran itself immune to the "people power" wave sweeping the Arab world, or will the Iranian pro-democracy movement be able to ride the regional wave that they themselves arguably sparked in June 2009?

If we depart from the assumption that the recent developments in the region present a challenge to one of Iran's main sources of regional soft power in the long-term, then Tehran's view of the United States and Israel may be less relevant compared to Iranian maneuvering vis-à-vis Turkey. For some years now, Tehran has viewed Washington—and also, by extension, Tel Aviv—as declining powers in the region. The reluctance of hard-liners in Iran to negotiate with the United States is not rooted necessarily in an ideological opposition to the idea of talking to or having relations with Washington, but rather, in the fear that any relationship with the United States would entail Iran adopting policies in the region similar to those of the Mubarak regime in Cairo. That is, Tehran would lose its independence and be forced to follow America's lead in investing in the Arab regimes rather than the Arab street. Since the Iranian hard-liners calculated that the Arab street would ultimately overthrow the monarchial and pro-American regimes in the region, Iran would best achieve its long-term security by aligning itself with the street. Consequently, it would contradict Iran's long-term security interest in the region to agree to any engagement with Washington that would be on America's terms and designed to rehabilitate Iran as a compliant U.S. ally.

This is in addition to the deep suspicions Iran's hard-liners have both of Washington's intentions when it comes to Iran and of the Obama administration's ability to muster the domestic support needed to bring about any real change in America's approach to Iran. President Obama had been disappointed in the cool response the Iranian leadership gave to his outreach in early 2009. On that occasion, the Iranians complained that slogans and nice words were insufficient to break the U.S.-Iranian deadlock, as were changes in America's posture that seemed to be only tactical. Only a strategic shift by Washington could unlock the U.S.-Iranian stalemate, they argued. In response to Obama's unprecedented Nowruz message in March 2009, Iran's Supreme Leader Ayatollah Ali Khamenei questioned the nature of the change Obama had offered, saying:

> They have the slogan of change . . . . Where is the change? What has changed? Clarify this to us. What changed? Has your enmity toward the Iranian nation changed? What signs are there to support this? Have you released the possessions of the Iranian nation? Have you removed the cruel sanctions? Have you stopped the insults, accusations, and negative propaganda against this great nation and its officials? Have you stopped your unconditional support for the Zionist regime? What has changed? They talk of change, but there are no changes in actions. We have not seen any changes . . . . Changes in words are not adequate; although we have not seen much of a change there either. Change must be real.[5]

---

5. Juan Cole, March 23, 2009, "OSC: Khamenei's Speech Replying to Obama," Informed Comment, http://www.juancole.com/2009/03/osc-khameneis-speech-replying-to-obama.html.

Obama's engagement did not bear any immediate fruit. From the perspective of the hard-liners in Iran, this was due to Obama's inability to muster real, strategic change in America's policy vis-à-vis Iran. Mindful of Tehran's self-perception of strength and its view of America as a sunset power, the Iranian hard-liners were not in favor of giving up one of Iran's strategic assets—its stockpile of low-enriched uranium—unless Iran received a strategic concession from the United States in turn. From the outset, Tehran was skeptical about Obama's abilities. Khamenei openly expressed his doubt as to whether Obama was in charge of America's foreign policy. "I would like to say that I do not know who makes decisions for the United States, the President, the Congress, elements behind the scenes?" he asked rhetorically, though he offered to change if Washington would change first. "We do not have any experience with the new American president and government. We'll see and judge. You change and we will change as well," he said.[6]

By now, the Iranian hard-liners' view of the United States as a desperately declining power in the region, incapable of shifting its policies in accordance to the new distribution of power in the region, seems to have cemented. In the last round of nuclear talks in Istanbul in January 2011,

*. . . the preference of the Iranian hard-liners will likely be to discard any notion of cooperation with the United States and instead opt to hasten Washington's ultimate exit from the region.*

Tehran took a surprisingly hard stance and even demanded the lifting of all sanctions and the right to enrich in order for talks to continue. The Iranian stance took Washington by surprise, but seemed to reflect Iran's confidence and its perception of strength vis-à-vis the United States. This confidence—or overconfidence—seemed to be rooted in three key developments.

6. Ibid.

First, although sanctions on Iran have harmed the Iranian economy and furthered Iran's international isolation, they have not changed Iran's calculations. As a result, Iran has withstood the pressure and Washington has wasted one of its last cards. The Obama administration's ability to muster a new round of UN sanctions within the next twelve months is limited. Thus, Iran believes that it is in a stronger position compared to the United States since Washington has fewer cards to play with while Iran's nuclear program continues to grow, albeit at a relatively slow pace. Second, the combination of higher oil prices and the gasoline subsidy reform that the Ahmadinejad administration has implemented has left the Iranian government with more cash in hand, at least in the short run. Finally, while the Obama administration has succeeded in isolating Iran on the international scene, Iran is paradoxically less isolated regionally. Even prior to the fall of Mubarak, Iran had scored important victories in both Iraq and Lebanon and strengthened its regional position.

Thus, going forward, the preference of the Iranian hard-liners will likely be to discard any notion of cooperation with the United States and instead opt to hasten Washington's ultimate exit from the region. This will not mean that Iran will spurn opportunities for tactical collaboration with the United States. On the contrary, Iran's interest in tactical collaboration with Washington may increase as its certainty in America's decline grows. As Washington's influence wanes, Iran's confidence in dealing with the United States in a manner that will not lead to Iran's subjugation and loss of independence may increase. Ongoing informal talks between the United States and Iran seem to suggest that the Iranians are eager to deal with the United States in Afghanistan and surprisingly accepted the American condition that those talks not be linked to the nuclear issue. Nevertheless, even as Iran engages Washington tactically, its strategic objective will likely still be to further weaken the United States and precipitate its eventual military departure from the region. Unlike the reformists and their apparent idea of a partnership with the United States, the hard-liners appear to seek a "codified rivalry" with the United States. This type of rivalry will enable Iran to continue to amass soft power in the region by maintaining the role of the region's premier critic of the United States, while ensuring that the rivalry between the two countries does not spill over into an open military confrontation. Within the context of such a rivalry, tactical collaboration is permitted as long as it does not contradict the strategic objective of ensuring America's military exit.

A recent historical parallel exists that exemplifies the type of engagement with which Iran's supreme leader seems comfortable. In 2001, in the aftermath of the September 11 terrorist attacks, Washington and Tehran collaborated extensively in Afghanistan in order to topple the Taliban government. James Dobbins, the president's special envoy for Afghanistan, led the American delegation. He has recounted how, contrary to the common perception in Washington, the United States did not assemble a coalition against the Taliban; Washington joined an existing coalition led by Iran. Meeting in Geneva, the U.S.-Iranian discussions focused on how to effectively unseat the Taliban and establish an Afghan government. Iranian diplomats impressed their American and European counterparts with their knowledge and expertise about Afghanistan and the Taliban—and Iran's material help was not negligible. The Iranians offered airbases to the United States, offered to perform search and rescue missions for downed American pilots, served as a bridge between the Northern Alliance and the Americans in the campaign against the Taliban, and on occasion even used information provided by American forces to find and kill fleeing al-Qaeda leaders.[7]

Nowhere was this common interest clearer than at the Bonn Conference of December 2001, where a number of prominent Afghans and representatives from various countries, including the United States and Iran, met under UN auspices to develop a plan for governing Afghanistan. The United States and Iran carefully laid the groundwork for the conference weeks in advance. Iran's political clout with warring Afghan groups proved crucial. While Washington and Tehran were on the same side, Iran's influence over the Afghans—not American threats and promises—was what moved the negotiations forward.

Yet, while the United States and Iran were closely collaborating and Iran was even pushing the U.S. side to use more force against the Taliban, Khamenei still used every opportunity to blast America's aggression against Afghanistan and its invasion of Muslim lands. Iran's hard-line leader was collaborating with the United States and benefitting from American military intervention, but he was not willing to give up his anti-American posture because of the sense that the Islamic Republic's soft power among the key constituency of the Arab and Muslim masses was dependent on it remaining a vocal critic of the United States.

---

7. Kenneth Pollack, *The Persian Puzzle* (New York: Random House, 2004), pp. 346–347.

If this notion of soft power is of such central importance to the Iranian leadership, then arguably the greatest challenge Iran will face going forward is the emergence of a new foreign policy orientation in the region by states that traditionally have been following America's lead. Turkey and Egypt will no longer play a role pliant to U.S. preferences. If these countries continue being assertive, then Iran will lose some of its uniqueness and one of its main sources of soft power may be at risk. These threats to Iran appear more likely when you consider these factors: the greater confidence among the new Arab leaders, an Arab youth less concerned with Iran—which they increasingly associate with the old picture—and the fact that Turkey is a formidable competitor in this region. Turkey is a part of the G20, a member of the current Security Council, and a nation with a booming economy. Iran, by contrast, is not part of any of these clubs. Imagine if the flotilla had been Iranian and not Turkish—would there have been a Security Council meeting to discuss it? Turkey even has soft power in Iran itself. Many Iranians travel to Turkey without visas to unwind, and a quarter of the Iranian population speaks a dialect of Turkish. Furthermore, unlike Iran, Turkey has other sources of soft power in the region, including cultural affinity and expansive economic ties, which may present Iran with a major challenge in future competitions for regional leadership between Tehran and Ankara.[8] Turkish Prime Minister Tayyip Erdoğan's outbursts against Israel—as well as concrete Turkish efforts to put Israel on the defensive—have won the Turks much admiration among the Arab masses. Already, the Iranians have been somewhat annoyed with Ankara's ability to "hijack" the anti-Israel card from Tehran. One observer in Tehran quipped that Iran had done all the groundwork "in the resistance against Israel," and then in the last minute the Turks stole the show and got all the credit.

There is an assumption that ultimately the relationship between Turkey and Iran will be a competition. If that is the case, what will be the balance between collaboration and competition? They have been competing in Iraq and are maintaining a mature relationship, indicating a tame competition between the two. In this context, there is something to be said about the Turkish-Iranian nuclear deal—not about the impact of sanctions or fear of war, but about competing with Iran and handling

8. See, for instance, the effect of Turkish soap operas on the Arab population. Nadia Bilbassy-Charters, "Leave It to Turkish Soap Operas to Conquer Hearts and Minds," *Foreign Policy*, April 15, 2010.

the decline of U.S. power in the region. If there had been an agreement, then Turkey would have been able to constrain Iran, while maintaining their competition with a web of other agreements. Additionally, it might be a healthy thing to have this competition since Iran, as a country that is becoming increasingly authoritarian, would be at a huge disadvantage vis-à-vis Turkey, a country with one of the only successful democracies in the region.

Although Iran has longed for the post-American era in the region, the current regional situation may paradoxically present Iran with a more arduous challenge than anticipated. Despite the significant ideological flexibility shown by the Islamic Republic in the past, its ability to adjust to this new reality seems limited.

# 11

# The Iranian Factor: Comments and Discussion

## *Ruhi Ramazani:*

Trita Parsi has rightly assessed Iran's relationship toward the United States, Turkey, and Israel and correctly talked about Iran and the United States in terms of American containment. However, Parsi seems to blame the hard-liners for Iran's conflict and poor relationship with the United States, but I am convinced that Iran and the United States cannot get together for one fundamental reason. Since the 1979 Revolution, the Iranians have never been convinced that the United States was not focusing on changing their regime. In fact, the reason for taking the Americans hostage was because they believed the Americans were bringing the Shah back. Iranians do not believe America on any issue—they think that ultimately the interest of the United States is regime change. When Khamenei said, "You change and we will change," he meant a recognition of Iran by the United States—one not given to Iran since the Shah. In Iran, the nuclear issue is perceived as an excuse for the United States, which never liked the post-1979 Iranian regime, to change it.

In terms of the Arab world, no one can predict the outcomes of the purportedly pro-democracy uprisings in the broader Middle East from Tunisia to Bahrain, mainly because they are still in progress. Trita Parsi has given us a thoughtful assessment of the impact of this environment of upheaval on Iran, Israel, and the United States. He has focused primarily on the complex, emerging effects of the uprisings on the rivalry between the United States and Israel, on the one hand, and Iran on the other.

Gazing into the future, however, I envisage the impact of the current turbulent circumstances on the emergence of a new triangle of rivalry among Iran, Turkey, and Egypt. It is probable that post-Mubarak Egypt will make a bid for regional preeminence as Iran and Turkey are now

*I envisage the emergence of a new triangle of rivalry among Iran, Turkey, and Egypt.*

doing. The changing dynamics of the regional situation could help or hinder the prospects of achieving regional leadership by Iran, Turkey, and Egypt. I think on balance, however, that in the short term these three regional powers will have more to gain than lose in power and influence in the Middle East by competing with one another. To explain, I will take up each of the three major players in turn.

1. **Iran:** Iran's ancient bid for regional preeminence and its growing influence could benefit from the current turbulent situation because of a variety of factors, including the following:

- The downfall of Mubarak, who staunchly supported the U.S. policy of containment and isolation of Iran, would benefit Tehran. The Egyptian and Iranian foreign ministers have already signaled the interest of their nations in resuming diplomatic relations.
- Iran would welcome the prospect of the cold peace between Israel and Egypt turning colder.
- Reduced chances of peace between Syria and Israel would strengthen Tehran's alliance with Damascus.
- The peace between Jordan and Israel could become lukewarm, to Iran's advantage.
- The withdrawal of U.S. forces from Iraq in 2011 and from Afghanistan in 2014 would increase Iran's influence in Kabul and Baghdad.

2. **Turkey:** The AKP's bid for regional primacy could intensify from a whole variety of factors, including the following ones:

- Turkey could set itself up as the democratic role model for the rest of the Muslim Middle East, though some analysts claim that under the guise of democracy promotion the AKP is actually projecting an Islamist model.

- Turkey's ties with the Muslim Brotherhood in Egypt could deepen now that the ban on the Muslim Brotherhood's participation in elections is lifted. Besides being the best-organized group, the Muslim Brotherhood is politically the most experienced faction; it participated in Egyptian elections with candidates running as independents during the Mubarak era.
- The possible reconciliation between Hamas and the Palestinian Authority could deepen Turkey's longstanding pro-Palestinian stance, which resonates to the Arab street. .
- Turkey's good-neighbor policy could expand as more Arab states adopt proactive foreign policies that are less dependent on the United States.
- Turkey's deteriorating relations with Israel would probably deepen in the new context of the Arab awakening.

3. **Egypt:** Post-Mubarak Egypt would reassert its claim to leadership in the Arab world. It is viewed as the most influential Arab state for historical, cultural, and political reasons.

- Egypt would adopt a more independent foreign policy from the United States.
- Egypt's cold peace with Israel could become colder. Egypt would keep its agreement with Israel, but with even less enthusiasm than previously.
- Egypt would drop its support of America's containment policy toward Iran. The Egyptian interim government allowed the passage of Iranian ships through the Suez Canal, an unprecedented event since the Iranian Revolution of 1979. As said before, the foreign ministers of Iran and Egypt have said their countries would want to resume diplomatic relations.
- The rise of the Muslim Brotherhood in Egyptian politics would resonate to the Muslim Brotherhood groups in Jordan and elsewhere in the Middle East.
- Transition of Egypt to a possible democratic and pluralistic polity could make it a role model for the Arab world.

## Looking Ahead

The gaining of influence by Iran, Turkey, and Egypt in their rivalry for regional primacy would be an important development in the short term. In the long term, however, there is no guarantee that they would be able to sustain power and project influence in the Muslim Middle East.

I say there is no guarantee based on a key lesson of the Iranian experience. The Shah's regime enjoyed significant regional and even global influence. His regional ambition stretched from the Persian Gulf and the Middle East all the way to the Pacific Ocean. Nevertheless, Iran's power collapsed and the Shah's dream of a "Great Civilization" vanished because the regime had failed for decades to make needed social, economic, and political reforms before the eruption of the Iranian Revolution in 1979. That is the lesson for other rising powers in the region: If they do not address domestic aspirations for freedom and better standards of living, then they will be ephemeral in the long term.

## *Farzaneh Milani:*

I believe literature has always been, and is more and more, relevant to Iranian politics. Without relying on patterns of the past or theories about the future, our literature has captured the essence of Iran's struggle for

*. . . Iranian writers have paid close attention to the streets and they have reflected more accurately the political realities than the overwhelming majority of our politicians and political scientists.*

democracy, gender equity, and human rights. It has epitomized the chaos and vibrancy of a culture in search of its identity. It has depicted a nation in the process of redefining itself. It has indeed offered a multilayered portrait, from the street level to the pulpit, the kind of history and politics you will not see in history or political science books; nonetheless, the kind of history and politics that are vital in better understanding Iran. I do agree with Enrique Vila-Matas, the Spanish novelist, that "Literature, as much as we delight in denying it, allows us to recall from oblivion all that which the contemporary eye, more immoral every day, endeavours to pass over with absolute indifference."

In discussing the complex relations between Iran, Israel, Turkey, and the United States, Trita Parsi points out astutely that the streets will surely dictate the future course of events in Iran. I fully agree with that assertion. I also want to suggest that Iranian writers have paid closer attention to the streets in Iran for the last several decades and that as a consequence they have reflected more accurately the political realities there than, may I dare say, the overwhelming majority of our politicians and political scientists. For instance, while, to the best of my knowledge, our political analysts rarely saw what was coming in 1979, prescient Iranian writers predicted the revolution with uncanny clarity. They also talked about it not from the safe space of the Diaspora, but from within the country itself.

At a time when political leaders of the country believed themselves invincible and at the height of their powers, when exceptionally few, either in or outside the country, foresaw a change of regime, let alone a revolution, Iranian writers anticipated a seismic change and the end of 2,500 years of dynastic and imperial rule. As early as the mid-1960s, the poet Forugh Farrokhzad predicted a revolution that would shake the foundation of Iranian society.

In a poem aptly titled, "I Feel Sorry for The Garden," she wrote, "All day long / the sounds of blasts and explosions can be heard. / Instead of flowers / our neighbors plant mortars and machine guns in their garden / they store gunpowder in their covered pools. / the kids in our neighbourhood / fill their backpacks with little bombs."

Writer and film director Ibrahim Golestan went even further. At the height of the Shah's power, in the mid-1970s, he foretold with eerie precision the crumbling of the regime and portrayed its downfall in his book, *Mysteries of the Treasure of Ghost Valley*. Golestan's message seemed so utterly unrealistic, so thoroughly unimaginable, that the clueless authorities did not even bother to censor his book or the film based on it.

Immediately after the 1979 Revolution, it was Iranian writers again who witnessed the grisly brutality that had so quickly taken hold of their society. Although many of them did support the revolution, they were the ones who had the courage to portray the new rulers as hatchet men, committed to extending their bloody control in every direction. They were the ones who saw, in the thrust of the rulers' daggers, in the crack of their whips, in their contempt for elegance and beauty, a chilling lust for power and violence. They saw the country's new leaders as executioners of light, love, and freedom, as assassins of the smile, as thugs who mercilessly burned books, jasmine, and innocent canaries. Ahmad Shamlu wrote in

1980, "In this crooked dead end of cold / they kindle fire / fueled with songs and poems / it is a strange time, my love."

I often wonder what would have happened in the earliest days of the revolution, when the country was embroiled in the seizure of the American Embassy, if our political theoreticians had joined ranks with the writers in our country. I ask myself whether Iranian history might have taken a different course, if our politicians and political scientists, instead of celebrating the struggle against dynastic rule, imperialism, and foreign intervention, had chosen to add their voices to those of rebellious Iranian writers who were protesting the trampling of basic human rights? What if they had focused not only on the iron fist that had taken the Americans hostage in their embassy, but also on the chains that were encircling their own lives and those lives of the Iranian people more and more every day?

Parsi asks, "Will the Iranian pro-democracy movement be able to ride the regional wave that they themselves arguably sparked in June 2009?" Let me answer in my concluding remarks by turning to the crystal ball of Iranian literature and repeating the words of the poet Simin Behbahani. Behbahani: the iconic face of resistance; the eloquent voice of dissent; the 83-year-old woman whose passport has been confiscated and who is virtually under country arrest.

> I am no twig to bend easily
> I am the tall, unyielding pine tree
> In me is the essence of resistance
> Even if I am cut into pieces.

The Iranian people's desire for democracy, their claim on human rights, and their belief in human dignity is no twig to bend easily. Look at the massive and desegregated demonstrations of Iranian women and men facing bullets and batons with open hands and life-affirming words. Then, rest assured this movement, like the words of our writers and poets, cannot be handcuffed. It cannot be arrested, jailed, or murdered. It is unyielding.

## Discussion:

**William Quandt:** Some conservative Israeli strategic thinkers openly treat Iran as a bombing target and little more. They contend that if the United States does not preemptively bomb Iran, then Iran will succeed in dominating the Middle East as a nuclear power. These thinkers believe that the events in Egypt have actually aggravated this situation because the fall of President Mubarak has left a regional power vacuum. With this in mind, how widespread among Americans who deal with Iran is the idea that a military confrontation with Iran is inevitable because of its emerging nuclear capabilities?

**Questioner:** If it is true, as some articles claim, that Iran is an existential threat to Israel and the United States, then what import does this idea have for the future of our relationships?

**Trita Parsi:** Questions of military intervention and nuclear weapons in Iran have been increasing again, in part because Israel is in a strategic dilemma. Over the last 30 years, Israel has lost three of its biggest allies in the region: Iran, Turkey, and the Mubarak regime in Egypt, and all of this has coincided with a time when Israel and the U.S. have diverging perspectives concerning the region. All of these factors have created a greater sense of fear among Israelis. It is also important to point out that the previous frame of the region as an existential struggle between a tyrannical, dictatorial state such as Iran and a Western-style, liberal democracy such as Israel was a comfortable, beneficial frame for Israel. Now Israel desperately aims to resurrect this frame as the region and its events continue to shatter it.

I have not come across many in the Israeli government who consider Iran an existential threat in and of itself. Instead, a combination of factors creates an extremely difficult situation for Israel; whether it is that the Iranians have a nuclear capability and the Israelis do not want to live under that umbrella, or that with a nuclear Iran, Israel risks losing some of its maneuverability in the region. For instance, with a nuclear Iran, can Israel enter Lebanon and still enjoy impunity? Will an Iranian nuclear capability threaten Israel's already struggling demographics by provoking people to leave the country? It is the combination of these factors along with a reduced American capability in the region that has persuaded many in the U.S. government to sympathize with Israel's view of Iran as an existential threat. It is not that Iran would use a nuclear weapon the moment it obtained one, or even ever, that worries Israel as much as it is the decline of American power in the region. Israel is losing, not gaining, friends.

In terms of Washington, there is an unspoken sense that a nuclear bomb in Iran is inevitable and we have opted for a containment policy not because it will work, but because it delays the problem. The United States does not have the political will to invest sufficiently in preventing a nuclear Iran through diplomacy. We could, but it would require an incredible amount of political capital in Washington and an equal willingness in Iran. The combination of these factors makes it tricky for any administration to tackle this when it looks at affairs in terms of no more than two years—the length of the congressional election cycle.

**Ruhi Ramazani:** I have seen reports indicating some people in the Israeli military do not believe Iran is an existential threat. What do you think?

**Trita Parsi:** It is almost embarrassing for Israelis to argue that Iran would be an existential threat, because Israel itself has a large arsenal of nuclear weapons. Once again, it is not the point of what Iran would do with a nuclear weapon, but the combination of all these factors. Furthermore, many individuals in the Israeli military have told me on the record that

---

*...many individuals in the Israeli military have told me that Iran is not an existential threat, but it is the organizing principle for foreign policy.*

---

Iran is not an existential threat, but it is the most prominent concern for Israel right now, as well as its organizing principle for foreign policy. It is not a threat perception that Israelis will easily give up, especially in a time when the region is unsettled.

**Ruhi Ramazani:** It is true the United States officially says it is not interested in Iranian regime change, but earlier I was referring to the Iranian perception, which remains convinced that from the very beginning there has been a U.S. inclination to see regime change in Iran. The Iranians believe that every sanction and UN Security Council decision, from the time of Jimmy Carter onward, represent various approaches the United States has engaged to encourage regime change. Iranians find further confirmation of their beliefs in statements made by Western leaders like Tony Blair that assert the Iranian nuclear matter is an important challenge, but the real challenge is the nature of the Iranian regime.

**William Quandt:** The Iranian perception has not been totally wrong concerning U.S. intentions toward Iran. For instance, when the United States labeled Iran as part of the "axis of evil" during Khatami's presidential term, it sent a signal that Washington thought the Iranian regime had to go. There have been strong expressions and different types of pressure indicating a U.S. desire for a new order in Iran. This is not just rhetoric, there are also actions to back it up.

On the nuclear issue, it is possible that the Israelis do not believe Iran is an existential threat, but some of these conservative Israeli strategic thinkers claim that if Iran acquires a nuclear weapon, then deterrence will not work. They argue this because Iran will not have a "second-strike capability," which is what made deterrence work in the U.S.-USSR context when both sides had this capability. Therefore, if Iran obtains the weapon, then they will have to "use it or lose it." If they do not use it, then Israel will take it out. In sum, it is not necessarily the issue that Israel would be hit, but that it seems like deterrence would not be a viable option like it was in the U.S.-USSR context.

**Gregory Gause:** The U.S.-USSR second-strike capability did not emerge until the 1960s, and yet nobody bombed anyone else . . . . Perhaps there might be a different way to understand Iran's soft power to mobilize public opinion in the Arab world on Arab-Israeli issues. It seems like Iranian influence in the Arab world is confined to places with very weak states. In these weak states, Iran, through its ideological, political, and sometimes financial connections with substate actors, can establish direct relations with these substate actors and through them affect the politics in that state. Lebanon serves as a classic example of this type of weak state, in addition to Iraq after 2003 and the Palestinian Authority—which is like a state and very weak. In other parts of the Arab world, Iranian influence might ebb and flow with public opinion, but has very little influence on how the state actually behaves. This makes Iran's strength in the Arab world its ability to influence substate actors in weak states, rather than its ability to represent the rejectionist stance on Arab-Israeli issues. What do you think of this explanation?

**Questioner:** One word has been missing so far in the discussions of the U.S. and Iran, which is engagement. It is implied that engagement must happen, but we keep making excuses that we are waiting for Iran to change first—do you have a quick thought on that? You mentioned it would be extremely difficult, but what are the elements in your vision to get this back on track?

**Trita Parsi:** Although Gause made an important point, I would rather explain Iran's strength in the region as a combination of different factors. Iran did not have access to some of the Arab states, but nevertheless, through its political posture, Iran managed to move from a situation where the Mubarak regime viewed it as the top problem in the region to one where only 9 percent of the Egyptian population views Iran as a problem. Now, did that translate into Iranian influence? No; there, Gause's other factor comes into play, Iran did not have any access—well it tried to, but they did not manage to obtain it. They could not exploit other weaknesses in the state, but they did exploit that political weakness. It is essentially an influence that is qualitatively different from the type of influence that the Turks, for instance, have been able to exert through their soft power.

On the question of engagement, it would be quite erroneous to believe that diplomacy in any way, shape, or form has been exhausted, even if some of the Obama administration's actions right now indicate that they have drawn this conclusion—at least for the rest of the first term. The administration walked in with a very genuine, honest vision and really did try at the beginning. Nevertheless, from the very first moment when the president took office, various interests, both domestic and foreign, kept compromising that vision. For example, there was a lot of pushback from allies in the region, including not only Israel, but also Saudi Arabia and other Arab states. The ultimate compromise, however—when the administration knew that they only had 12 months to secure some form of success to build on and create the political space to pursue engagement further—was what the Iranian regime itself did with the 2009 elections. This situation left the administration with essentially a short period—no more than three meetings or so—during late 2009 to try engagement earnestly. Their efforts ended up being diplomacy with one cast of the dice: If it worked, it worked; if it did not, it did not, and they would have to move on because there was not enough political space to try again.

This leads to the issue of the Turkish-Brazil nuclear deal. Everyone knows the general argument that the deal failed because 1,200 kilos of low-enriched uranium (LEU) was not enough, the Iranians were doing 20 percent, and so on, but ultimately the decisive factor was that the administration's political space ran out. Congress, which at the beginning had been skeptical of Obama's approach, had turned hostile by late 2009 and pushed the administration to pursue sanctions. The administration never dared to challenge Congress on this issue because of the consequences it would have on the Democratic Party in the November elections in 2010. It was not a battle they were willing to fight. Then, by the time you had the May 2010 agreement and the Tehran Declaration, getting sanctions had essentially turned into the administration's organizing principle for alliance management. They resolved that the way to keep every country on the same page was through sanctions, and that function took higher priority than actually seeing if the deal would work. This decision ultimately hurt the Turks and Brazilians because they were the eager parties to this deal who had worked hard to negotiate with Iran. Nevertheless, the administration chose sanctions and we are where we are right now.

I think engagement is still possible, but it will take time before any new opportunity arises, and when that opportunity comes I hope the administration will not choose to miss it.

**William Quandt:** Let us hope. Once again domestic politics has trumped strategic thinking.

# Glossary and Dramatis Personae

**Ahmadinejad, Mahmoud:** President of Iran since 2005.

**al-Asad, Bashar:** President of Syria, 2000 to present.

**al-Asad, Hafez:** President of Syria, 1970-2000.

**Arafat, Yasser:** Palestinian nationalist leader of PLO from 1968 to his death in 2004.

**Barak, Ehud:** Prime minister of Israel, 1999-2001; minister of defense since 2009.

**Ben Gurion, David:** Prime minister of Israel, 1948-1953, 1955-1963, from the Labor Party.

**Ben-Eliezer, Binyamin:** Former Israeli minister of defense, negotiator with Turkey 2010.

**Cem, Ismail:** Turkish foreign minister, 1997-2002.

**Davutoğlu, Ahmet:** Foreign minister of Turkey since 2009.

**Democratic Left Party (DSP):** Turkish political party led by Bülent Ecevit.

**Ecevit, Bülent:** Turkish prime minister, most recently 1999-2002, Democratic Left Party.

**Erbakan, Necmettin:** Turkish Islamist leader, briefly served as prime minister in 1996-97 before being ousted by military.

**Erdoğan, Recep Tayyip:** Turkish prime minister since 2002, AK Party.

**Foundation for Human Rights and Freedoms and Humanitarian Relief (IHH):** Turkish nongovernmental organization active in organizing *Mavi Marmara*-led flotilla to break Gaza blockade in 2010.

**Gül, Abdullah:** Turkish president since 2007 and minister of foreign affairs from 2003–07.

**Hamas:** Islamist Palestinian political party that won legislative elections in 2006 and controls Gaza.

**Hizbollah:** Lebanese political party led by Hassan Nasrallah, primarily strong among Shiite community, and with close ties to both the Asad regime in Syria and the Islamic Republic of Iran.

**Hussein, Saddam:** Iraqi leader from 1989 until his overthrow by American forces in 2003.

**Justice and Development Party (*Adalet ve Kalkınma Partisi*-AKP):** Turkish political party with roots in political Islam, in power since 2002.

**Khamenei, Ayatollah Ali:** President of Iran, 1989 to present.

**Khatami, Mohammad:** President of Iran, 1997-2005.

**Kurdistan Workers Party (PKK):** Outlawed radical Kurdish movement led by Abdullah Öcalan.

**Lieberman, Avigdor:** Foreign minister of Israel, 2009 to present, from right-wing Yisrael Beiteinu Party.

**Livni, Tzipi:** Foreign minister of Israel in Kadima-led government of Ehud Olmert, 2006-2009.

**Menderes, Adnan:** Prime minister of Turkey, 1950-60, hanged after military coup of 1960.

**Meshal, Khaled:** Damascus-based leader of Hamas's political wing.

**Motherland Party (ANAP):** Center-right Turkish political party identified with Turgut Özal, prime minister and then president of Turkey from 1983 to 1993.

**Mubarak, Hosni:** President of Egypt, 1982-2011.

**Muslim Brotherhood (Al-Ikhwan):** Egyptian Islamist movement.

**Nasrallah, Hassan:** Lebanese Shiite leader of Hizbollah party.

**National Action Party (MHP):** Right-wing Turkish nationalist party that gained thirteen percent of popular vote in 2011 election.

**Netanyahu, Benjamin:** Prime minister of Israel and chairman of the Likud party.

**Öcalan, Abdullah:** Leader of the Kurdish Workers Party, in prison since 1999.

**Olmert, Ehud:** Prime minister of Israel, 2006-2009.

**Özal, Turgut:** Turkish prime minister and president from 1983 to 1993, who set Turkish economy of liberal reform path.

**Palestine Liberation Organization (PLO):** Widely recognized Palestinian national movement led from 1968 by Yasir Arafat until 2004, then by Mahmoud Abbas.

**Palestinian Authority (PA):** Elected government of Palestinians in the West Bank and Gaza under terms of the Oslo Accord (1993).

**Peres, Shimon:** Long-time Israeli politician, currently president of Israel.

**Qaddafi, Muammar:** Libyan ruler, 1969–2011.

**Republican People's Party (CHP):** Secular nationalist party identified with founding of the Turkish Republic in 1923. Won twenty-six percent of the vote in 2011 election.

# About the Contributors

**Henri J. Barkey** is a visiting scholar in the Carnegie Endowment for International Peace Middle East Program and the Bernard L. and Bertha F. Cohen Professor at Lehigh University. He served as a member of the U.S. State Department Policy Planning Staff working primarily on issues related to the Middle East, the Eastern Mediterranean, and intelligence from 1998 to 2000. He has taught at Princeton, Columbia, the State University of New York, and the University of Pennsylvania. Barkey has authored, co-authored, and edited five books, among them *Turkey's Kurdish Question* with Graham Fuller, *Reluctant Neighbor: Turkey's Role in the Middle East*, and most recently, *European Responses to Globalization: Resistance, Adaptation and Alternatives*. His opinion editorials have appeared in *Newsweek*, *The Washington Post*, *The Wall Street Journal*, *Daily Star*, and *Los Angeles Times*, and he is a frequent guest on the *Newshour with Jim Lehrer* and *NPR*.

**Shlomo Brom** is a senior research fellow and the director of the Program on Israel-Palestinian Relations at the Institute for National Security Studies. He joined the Jaffee Center in 1998 after a long career in the Israeli Defense Forces (IDF). His most senior post in the IDF was director of the Strategic Planning Division in the Planning Branch of the General Staff. Brig. Gen. (ret.) Brom participated in peace negotiations with the Palestinians, Jordan, and Syria, and in Middle Eastern regional security talks during the 1990s. He continued to be involved in Track II dialogues on these subjects after his retirement from the IDF. In 2000, he was named deputy to the National Security Advisor. In 2005-2006, Brom was a member of the Meridor Committee established by the minister of defense to reexamine the security strategy and doctrine of the State of Israel. His primary areas of research are Israeli-Palestinian relations and national security doctrine. Brom authored *Israel and South Lebanon: In the Absence of a Peace Treaty with Syria*, and edited *The Middle East Military Balance*

*1999-2000* and *The Middle East Military Balance 2001-2002*. He is co-editor of *The Second Lebanon War: Strategic Dimensions.*

**F. Gregory Gause, III** is professor and chair of the Department of Political Science at the University of Vermont. He was director of the University's Middle East Studies Program from 1998 to 2008. In 2009-2010, he was the Kuwait Foundation Visiting Professor of International Affairs at the Kennedy School of Government, Harvard University. He was previously on the faculty of Columbia University (1987-1995) and was Fellow for Arab and Islamic Studies at the Council on Foreign Relations in New York (1993-1994). He has published three books—*The International Relations of the Persian Gulf* (Cambridge University Press, 2010); *Oil Monarchies: Domestic and Security Challenges in the Arab Gulf States* (Council on Foreign Relations Press, 1994); and *Saudi-Yemeni Relations: Domestic Structures and Foreign Influence* (Columbia University Press, 1990). His scholarly articles have appeared in *Foreign Affairs, Foreign Policy, Security Studies, Middle East Journal, Washington Quarterly, Journal of International Affairs, Review of International Studies,* and in other journals and edited volumes. He has testified on Gulf issues before Congressional committees and has made numerous appearances on television and radio commenting on Middle East issues.

**Yaprak Gürsoy** is currently an assistant professor at Istanbul Bilgi University. She received her PhD in 2008 from the University of Virginia, Department of Politics. She taught at Sabanci University in Turkey and Sciences Po Lille. Dr. Gürsoy's dissertation is a comparative study of Greece and Turkey on regime change, democratization, civil-military relations, and attitudes of businessmen toward regimes. For her dissertation, Dr. Gürsoy conducted more than 100 interviews with Greek and Turkish businessmen, politicians, and retired military officers. Her research in Salonika and Athens was funded by the State Scholarship Foundation of Greece. Her scholarly publications have appeared in the *East European Quarterly, Journal of Political and Military Sociology, Journal of Modern Greek Studies,* and *Turkish Studies.*

**Tina S. Kaidanow** assumed her duties as deputy assistant secretary in the Bureau of European and Eurasian Affairs in August 2009. In this capacity, Ms. Kaidanow is responsible for issues related to Greece, Turkey, Cyprus, and the Caucasus. Previously, she was the chief of mission and later the

U.S. ambassador to the Republic of Kosovo. Ms. Kaidanow served as the deputy chief of mission at the U.S. Embassy in Bosnia and Herzegovina from 2003 to 2006. Prior to that, she was the special assistant for European Affairs to Deputy Secretaries of State Strobe Talbott and Richard Armitage. A career member of the U.S. diplomatic service, Ambassador Kaidanow served as special assistant to U.S. Ambassador Christopher Hill in Skopje from 1998 to 1999, with specific responsibilities focused on the crisis in Kosovo, and had earlier assignments in Sarajevo (1997-1998) and Belgrade (1995-97). She has also held the position of director for Southeast European Affairs at the National Security Council.

**Ellen Laipson** is president and chief executive officer of the Stimson Center. She also directs the Southwest Asia project, which focuses on security issues in the Gulf region. Laipson joined the Stimson Center in 2002, after nearly 25 years of government service. Key positions included vice chair of the National Intelligence Council (NIC) (1997-2002), and special assistant to the U.S. permanent representative to the United Nations (1995-97). At the NIC, Laipson co-managed the interdisciplinary study "Global Trends 2015," and directed the NIC's outreach to think tanks and research organizations on a wide range of national security topics. Lampson's earlier government career focused on analysis and policy making on Middle East and South Asian issues. She was the director for Near East and South Asian Affairs for the National Security Council (1993-95), national intelligence officer for Near East and South Asia (1990-93), a member of the State Department's policy planning staff (1986-87), and a specialist in Middle East affairs for the Congressional Research Service.

**Jeffrey W. Legro** is the Randolph P. Compton Professor in the Woodrow Wilson Department of Politics at the University of Virginia. He is a cofounder and faculty associate of the Governing America in a Global Era Program at the Miller Center of Public Affairs. A specialist on international relations, Legro is the author of *Rethinking the World: Great Power Strategies and International Order* (2005) and *Cooperation under Fire: Anglo-German Restraint during World War II* (1995) and the editor (with Melvyn Leffler) of *To Lead the World: U.S. Strategy after the Bush Doctrine* (Oxford, 2008) and *In Uncertain Times: American Foreign Policy after the Berlin Wall and 9/11* (Cornell, 2011). Legro chaired the American Political Science Association (APSA) Task Force on U.S. Standing in the World and is past president of APSA's International History and Politics section. His articles on American foreign policy, international cooperation and conflict, China's future in world politics, international norms and law, military doctrine and strategy, and the causes of foreign policy ideas and national identity have appeared in *Foreign Policy*, *The American Political Science Review*, *International Organization*, *International Security*, *American Journal of Political Science*, *European Journal of International Relations*, and *Perspectives on Politics*. He is on the editorial board of the *Washington Quarterly*.

**Daniel Levy** is a senior research fellow and co-director of the Middle East Task Force at the New America Foundation and a senior fellow and director of the Prospects for Peace Initiative at The Century Foundation. He serves as a coeditor of *The Middle East Channel*, an online initiative of *Foreign Policy* magazine and the Project on Middle East Political Science at George Washington University together with NAF's Middle East Task Force. During the Barak Government of 1999-2001, Levy worked in the Israeli Prime Minister's Office as special adviser and head of Jerusalem Affairs. Mr. Levy was a member of the official Israeli delegation to the Taba negotiations with the Palestinians in January 2001, and previously served on the Israeli negotiating team to the "Oslo B" Agreement from May to September 1995, under Prime Minister Yitzhak Rabin. He also served as the lead Israeli drafter of the Geneva Initiative.

**Allen Lynch** is the director of research at the Center for International Studies and a professor in the Woodrow Wilson Department of Politics at the University of Virginia. His current research interests include Russian foreign policy, Russian politics in comparative perspective, and relationships between international order and political development. In 2006, he received an All-University Teaching Award at the University of Virginia. Professor Lynch is the author of more than 36 books and articles including: *How Russia is not Ruled: Reflections on Russian Political Development*; *Does Russia Have a Democratic Future?*; *Europe from the Balkans to the Urals: the Disintegration of Yugoslavia and the USSR and International Politics*; *The Cold War is Over? Again*; *Political and Military Implications of the Nuclear Winter Theory*; and *The Soviet Study of International Relations*. His articles have appeared in numerous journals including *Foreign Affairs*, *Foreign Policy*, *Europe-Asia Studies*, *Review of International Affairs*, and *Bulletin of the Atomic Scientists*, among many others.

**Farzaneh Milani** is the chair and professor of Middle Eastern and South Asian Languages and Cultures and Studies in Women and Gender at the University of Virginia. A past president of the Association of Middle Eastern Women Studies in America, Milani was the recipient of the All-University Teaching Award in 1998 and was nominated for Virginia Faculty of the Year in 1999. Milani is the author of *Veils and Words: The Emerging Voice of Iranian Women Writers*, and *A Cup of Sin: Selected Poems of Simin Behbahani* (with Kaveh Safa). She has published over 100 articles, epilogues, forewords, and afterwords in Persian and in English. She has served as the guest editor for two special issues of *Nimeye-Digar, Persian Language Feminist Journal* (on Simin Daneshvar and Simin Behbahani), *IranNameh* (on Simin Behbahani), and *Iranian Studies: Journal of the International Society for Iranian Studies* (on Simin Behbahani). She has written for *The New York Times, The Washington Post, The Christian Science Monitor, Ms. Magazine, Readers Digest, USA Today*, and NPR's *All Things Considered.*

**Soli Özel** is a professor of International Relations and Political Science at Istanbul Kadir Has University. Özel has also taught at U.C. Santa Cruz, the John Hopkins School of Advanced International Studies (SAIS), University of Washington, Hebrew University, and *Boğaziçi* University in Istanbul. He was a fellow at St. Antony's College at Oxford in the spring of 2002, and he was a senior visiting fellow at the European Union Institute for Security Studies in the fall of the same year. Özel's articles and opinion pieces appear in a wide variety of leading newspapers in Turkey and elsewhere around the world. Currently, he is a columnist for *Haberturk* newspaper, a frequent contributor to *The Washington Post's* "Post Global," and the former editor of the Turkish edition of *Foreign Policy*. Most recently, he co-authored the report "Rebuilding a Partnership: Turkish-American Relations For a New Era" with Dr. Suhnaz Yilmaz and Abdullah Akyuz.

**Trita Parsi** was the 2010 recipient of the Grawemeyer Award for Ideas Improving World Order. He is the founder and president of the National Iranian American Council and an expert on U.S. -Iranian relations, Iranian politics, and Middle East politics. He is the author of *Treacherous Alliance: The Secret Dealings of Iran, Israel and the United States,* for which he conducted more than 130 interviews with senior Israeli, Iranian, and American decision-makers. *Treacherous Alliance* was the silver medal winner of the 2008 Arthur Ross Book Award from the Council on Foreign Relations. Parsi's articles on Middle East affairs have been published in

*The Wall Street Journal, Financial Times, Jane's Intelligence Review, The Nation, The American Conservative, The Jerusalem Post, The Forward,* and others. He is a frequent guest on CNN, PBS's *Newshour with Jim Lehrer,* NPR, the BBC, and Al Jazeera.

**William B. Quandt** is the Edward R. Stettinius Professor of Politics in the Woodrow Wilson Department of Politics at the University of Virginia. From 2000 to 2003, he also served as Vice Provost for International Affairs at the University. He teaches courses on the Middle East and American Foreign Policy. Prior to this appointment, he was a senior fellow in the Foreign Policy Studies Program at the Brookings Institution, where he conducted research on the Middle East, American policy toward the Arab-Israeli conflict, and energy policy. Before going to Brookings in 1979, Dr. Quandt served as a staff member on the National Security Council (1972-1974, 1977-1979). He was actively involved in the negotiations that led to the Camp David Accords and the Egyptian-Israeli Peace Treaty. Dr. Quandt has written numerous books, and his articles have appeared in a wide variety of publications. His books include: *Peace Process: American Diplomacy and the Arab-Israeli Conflict Since 1967; Between Ballots and Bullets: Algeria's Transition from Authoritarianism; The United States and Egypt: An Essay on Policy for the 1990s; Camp David: Peacemaking and Politics; Saudi Arabia in the 1980s: Foreign Policy, Security, and Oil; Decade of Decisions: American Foreign Policy Toward the Arab-Israeli Conflict, 1967-1976;* and *Revolution and Political Leadership: Algeria, 1954-1968.* He also edited *The Middle East: Ten Years After Camp David.*

**Ruhi Ramazani** is professor emeritus in the Woodrow Wilson Department of Government and Foreign Affairs at the University of Virginia. Professor Ramazani immigrated from Iran to America in 1952. He is a founder of Iranian studies in America and has been referred to as "the Dean of Iranian Foreign Policy Studies in the United States." He has authored and edited a dozen books and more than 100 articles, some of which have been translated into Arabic, Persian, and Turkish. He has been a consultant on the Persian Gulf and Iran to the White House, the departments of State, Defense, and Treasury, and the United Nations Secretariat General and the foreign ministries of Israel, Britain, Spain, Iran, Turkey, and Pakistan.

**Brantly Womack** is the Cumming Memorial Professor of Foreign Affairs in the Woodrow Wilson Department of Politics at the University of Virginia. Dr. Womack is the author of *China among Unequals: Asymmetric Foreign Relations in Asia; China and Vietnam: The Politics of Asymmetry; Foundations of Mao Zedong's Political Thought, 1917-1935*; and co-author of *Politics in China* (3rd ed.). He is editor of *China's Rise in Historical Perspective, Contemporary Chinese Politics in Historical Perspective; Media and the Chinese Public; Electoral Reform in China*. In addition, Dr. Womack is author of more than one hundred journal articles and book chapters on Asian politics, including articles in *World Politics, World Policy Journal, China Quarterly, Pacific Affairs,* and *China Journal*. He has been a Fulbright Scholar, Woodrow Wilson Fellow, and Mellon Fellow and recipient of numerous research grants. He served as a honorary professor at Jilin University (Changchun, China), and at East China Normal University (Shanghai, China). Dr. Womack's current research interests include asymmetric international relationships; the relationship of public authority and popular power in China; provincial diversification in China; domestic politics and foreign policy of Vietnam; China's relations with Southeast Asia.

**Philip Zelikow** is the White Burkett Miller Professor and Director of Graduate Studies in History at the University of Virginia. Zelikow began his professional career as a trial and appellate lawyer in Texas. After further graduate study, he joined the U.S. Foreign Service and was posted overseas and in Washington, including service on the NSC staff for President George H.W. Bush. Since 1991, he has taught and directed research programs at Harvard University and at the University of Virginia. In addition to service on some government advisory boards, and as an elected member of a local school board, he has taken two public service leaves from academia to return full-time to government service, as director of the 9/11 Commission and later as counselor of the Department of State for Secretary Condoleezza Rice. He also advises the Bill & Melinda Gates Foundation's program in global development. In Fall 2009, he was a fellow at the American Academy in Berlin. He is working on a history of U.S. foreign policy begun by his late colleague, Ernest May.